STIGMA FIGHTERS

VOLUME 3

SARAH FADER

CONTENTS

INTRODUCTION

As a woman with schizophrenia who is constantly navigating the road to survival, that is exactly what the Stigma Fighters Anthology means to me. It is hundreds of voices, with so many more to come, surviving. Mental disorders are hard enough to survive even without the stigma attached, but these amazing people have survived both and use their voices as well as their lives, to tell the world that we can make it through the battle. We can live normal lives, rise above stigma, and we can contribute to society. We can live. We choose to live, and we do that despite the way we are treated by people who don't understand what we go through.

The candid people telling their stories in the Stigma Fighters Anthology not only do it for themselves but for others—others going through what they are. I don't know if the authors realize how powerful their stories are to others out there living with these same disorders, but our words are the difference between life and death; between happiness and sadness. With our words, we have chosen to dedicate our lives to our communities by writing these stories. We hope similarly suffering people will come across this anthology and choose to rise above their stigma because we could, and did. The Writers Advocate for the people and this anthology celebrates their ambition and bravery throughout these stories.

The stigma will not prevail because we see it and fight. We are the Stigma Fighters, and these are our stories.

-Allie Burke
    Executive Director, Stigma Fighters

FOREWORD

There is something empowering about telling our stories, even if we feel like it may only be a shout into the world's void. Telling your story, your way, can suddenly give you control of the narrative you felt someone else was controlling for so long.

However, reading stories from others is a completely different type of empowerment. It gives us hope and reminds us we aren't alone while offering us a chance to see into the world of someone who is also struggling. Reading different stories reveals a glimpse into illnesses we may not see or a point of view we may not have connected with before.

— COURTNEY KEESEE ADMINISTRATOR,
STIGMA FIGHTERS

TALKING TO MYSELF

MICHELLE HAMMER

THIS IS HARD TO EXPLAIN, and I'm not really sure how to do it, but I want to explain what it's like when I talk to myself. Everyone talks to themselves…well a little bit, but not like me. Not in the way I do it. They don't feel like they're in a different place, with different people. They know exactly what their reality is. But I'm gone. Zoned out. If you're trying to get my attention, it may take a minute. Then, I'll snap out of it, but at that point in time…I'm gone.

It became harder to hide as I got older, not that it was ever easy to hide… When I first went to college, I lived in a small quad dorm with three other roommates. I tried very hard to silence the talking, but there were those moments that I didn't realize I was speaking. My roommates noticed, but I just told them I was "thinking out loud." That excuse worked for a while. One time while I thought my roommate was sleeping, she heard me and told me, "wow, I could have sworn there was another person in the room the way you were talking."

I talk about a variety of things when I talk to myself. They fall into the broad categories of good or bad. When it's good, I often burst into laughter. My Sophomore year of college, I had a professor who called me up after class and asked me if I was laughing at him while he taught. I didn't know how to respond, so I just told him, "I just do that...sorry." When it's bad, though, it's terrible. I'm in a fight in my head. It's an argument that won't end. Tons of ruminating thoughts that just repeat and repeat, over and over again.

Thankfully, the bad ones don't happen to me much anymore, which I couldn't be happier about since I've had some various reactions over the years, especially while living in New York City. People have looked at me very strangely on the subway, and I know exactly why. They see me having a chat with an invisible person. I guess I deserved the strange looks they gave me. Although, I've had positive reactions too. Once, a woman told me I had a "Mona Lisa Smile." I must have had a good talk that day. Another time, a man in Starbucks told me that I have great energy and happiness. I guess I was having another good talk that day, too.

It's hard to talk about talking to myself. Sometimes I think there are things I wished would happen, or things I wished never happened, and I think about how I would have done things differently. But sometimes, those things I think of, never happened, and I don't know which are true and which aren't. Those situations make it hard to trust myself, and if I can't trust my own thoughts, then who can I trust? Fortunately, I have a supportive safety net; my family and friends—I know I can trust them. That's why I feel so lucky that I am where I am today.

About a year ago, I was on the F train sitting near a homeless man. He was talking to himself loudly while he was zoned out. I could tell he didn't know what was real, and, I thought about how much of myself I could see in him. Without all the help I've gotten, would I be on the streets? *I have to do something*, I thought then. *I have to make a change.* Mentally ill people need help and should not be living on the streets.

BEAUTIFULLY BROKEN

ABBIE ZEBROWSKI

"The hardest challenge is to be yourself in a world where everyone is trying to make you be somebody else."

— E.E. CUMMINGS

I REMEMBER FEELING different when I started third grade, as though there was an impenetrable glass wall between myself and my peers. I could see them, I could hear them, but I could not relate to them. Kids don't handle 'different' well and they were not kind to me. I was sensitive and became an easy target. Little did I know this was just the beginning of a lifelong battle between what was considered 'normal' and how my brain works.

I have struggled relating with others my whole life, but it wasn't until high school that I began to understand why. When I was about sixteen years old I was diagnosed with Major Depressive Disorder. I was officially different – certifiably different – from everyone else I knew. The diagnosis was a stepping stone to understanding it; though I couldn't really comprehend it at the time, those three words were (and are) the reason behind my struggles.

I wish it on no one and wonder what my life might be like if my brain produced the proper chemicals, yet I cannot dwell upon such fairy tales. Depression has shaped every curve, every groove, every move and choice of my life's journey. Depression does not define me but depression is a large part of me. To deny that fact would be to deny that I need oxygen to breathe. It is the passion that feeds my creative soul and it is the weight that holds me in the darkest of nights.

The depths of my lows are deeper than any sadness, which is more intense than anything you could imagine. It is beyond sadness. It is feeling as though there will never be light again, like the sun will never rise and there is no moon or stars in the sky. It is nothingness, complete emptiness – like trying to fill a bottomless glass.

I fought my diagnosis in the beginning. I was what the psychiatric community calls 'non-compliant' because I did not understand why I had to take a pill to be happy. None of my friends or family needed a pill to feel happiness, so why should I? It made me angry. Being different was not popular, fitting in was all I wanted – and I wanted it desperately. I did not understand that my brain and body was, when it came down to it, broken. So I would take the meds sporadically, not realizing this only made my condition worse. My life was, and to some extent still is, a constant emotional roller-coaster; a ride from which I will never be able to disembark.

Attempting to manage depression is a defeating, numbing, and terrifying experience. While there are a multitude of psychotropic medications on the market, there is very little science to determine which medication will work for a specific individual. I refer to it as the 'medication game', wherein psychiatrists take an educated guess based on a patient's diagnosis and then throw medications into the mix to see if they will alleviate the symptoms. More often than not, medications must be changed multiple times before the right 'cocktail' is found and the side effects can be worse than the original symptoms of the disease.

I have reached partial remission once. It lasted almost three years before my sanity started slipping away like sand between my fingers – slowly at first, and then as I tried to hold on tighter it slipped more rapidly away. I was hopeful that a slight tweak in the meds would save me, but it did the opposite. I was suicidal within a week. It has taken two years of playing the medication game, as well as trying Transcranial Magnetic Stimulation therapy, and finally a DNA test to determine which medications my body can actually metabolize, before finding medications that are starting to work.

The rest of the world may think I'm crazy because they don't know what it's like to fight for their sanity. My body tries to break me but I am unstoppable. My mind is both my worst enemy and my only hope. Depression swims through my blood, giving life to my words, like the marrow in my bones gives life to my body. This disease will never defeat me. Each broken piece of me is fucking beautiful. Even at my weakest, I am strong, for I am still here, breathing – the evidence of strength is in every additional beat of my heart.

Here's the craziest part of my whole story… I attended and graduated from college with a bachelor's degree. I met an amazing man I married and live with happily. I am a well-adjusted member of our society and an advocate, not only for myself, but for all people with mental health issues. I am a SUCCESS, by the world's terms, except somehow, having a mental illness negates every shred of it. The world defines me by my illness, in spite of everything I've accomplished.

Depression does not define me, but it is a large part of who I am. As much as I despise the disease, I love who I am and I wouldn't change that – even if the rest of the world would.

And dammit, I AM a success.

TINYLETTER.COM/CRYING

EVE PEYSER

I BEGAN SENDING out a newsletter every time I cried because I thought it would be funny. A compulsive journaler obsessed with keeping track of my various mental health issues—depression, anxiety, severe suicidal ideation, ADHD—I never had much desire to keep any of my mental health issues a secret. Talking about what I'm going through openly helps me overcome the worst, to release my emotions out so I can be free of their weight, to be not embarrassed about who I am. I wasn't sure who would want to get the email and what I would even say in them. But having to explain what's been going on with me over the past six months has helped me better understand why I feel the way I do, and who I am. Here's what happened [excerpted]:

* * *

9/8/16

subject: Teared Up

Life is hard.

---

* * *

9/13/16

subject: crying, unexpectedly

i was walking home, rushing because i have work, feeling anxious about picking the ideal food, a food i could stomach eating, a food i could desire because i've had issues with my appetite lately but feel really hungry — whatever besides the point — when a car full of men began catcalling me. it was flamboyant catcalling. loud and silly and performative. i think one of them howled "scooby dooby doo" at one point and there were a lot of "damns," comments about my body, etc.

i've been getting catcalled since i was quite literally 10-years-old — grew up in manhattan — i can handle it, BUT there was a group of sort of hipsterish looking guys walking toward me who witnessed the whole thing. being silently watched amplified the feeling of deep inhumanity that comes along with getting sexually harassed. there's a real humiliation to getting catcalled — an implicit understanding that, A. this might not be happening if i was dressed differently, and B. it's a reminder that, as a rule, strangers have no fucking respect for you for reasons that are largely outside of your control. i can usually swallow that. but having one group of men witness another group of men aggressively catcall me felt like shit, and not because i was looking for them to save me, just because having someone witness something, especially someone who is going to construe you as a victim, makes your innate victimhood more real. had women bore witness, at least they would understand.

then there's this anger that comes up with all this shit stealing away your time and energy — i walked a couple blocks out of my way because i didn't want to walk in the same direction as the car. i didn't end up getting food. i fucking spent time tweeting about it. then i started crying. then i wrote this fucking email. it took up a moderate portion of my time because i am who i am, for sure, but i want to be in control of how i spend my time.

anyways, the crying was brief and now it's over. i'm fine. i should order food and get to work now.

welp, suppose it's all right summer is ending. i love wearing shorts, but the repercussions of doing so almost seem not worth it.

until next time,

e

* * *

9/24/16

subject: cried a little bit in a bar last night

approximately half my sexual experiences from ages 15 to 20 were nonconsensual. i don't say this to shock anyone. it just comes with the territory of being a woman. you become sexually active; bad things happen. the thing no one tells you about getting sexually assaulted is that you're not always sure if it happened, if it was your fault, because sometimes, it sure feel like it partially is.

it's easier not to discuss sexual assault in this way. the

reason we talk about it in such black and white terms is because no one believes women when we say we got assaulted. what i mean to say is this:

I'm 18, visiting a friend from high school in Chicago, first time there and he's the only person i know, I'm more or less stuck with him. one night, he takes me to a party at his friend's apartment, where we'll sleep because it's in a supposedly unsafe neighborhood. my friend hasn't been particularly nice to me throughout my stay and I get tired-drunk at the party and go to sleep early. he comes into the bedroom hours later—we're sharing a bed, which is no big deal to me—to go to sleep. when he comes in, i realize I've fallen asleep with my very tight uncomfortable jeans on and I take them off and proceed to try to fall back asleep. suddenly, i feel him groping my breasts, reaching his hands around my underwear, and I'm frozen in shock. I say nothing. finally i muster the courage to grab my pants and go, but i'm in stuck in this frigidly cold stranger's apartment in an unfamiliar and i don't know anyone else there. (this is pre-iphone, like, damn.) i spend the night trying to sleep on the couch, using my coat as a blanket because i can't find one, shivering. i am so so trapped. the next day, we have breakfast, i say nothing. (was it my fault for taking off my jeans?)

that is, when it comes down to it, what i cried about last night. that trip to chicago certainly is a small bad thing that happened to me; it's certainly not the worst that's happened. the crazy thing? i was triggered by seeing the bed intruder meme video.

i cried about it last week too but didn't send out an email.

---

* * *

9/28/16

subject: cried all last night, crying now, will likely cry tomorrow

i feel cold and extremely alone and also lonely. i really don't enjoy being alive or my life and i'm very overwhelmed and i can't stop crying about it. i don't have much more to say. don't @ me.

love,
  eve

---

* * *

9/29/16

subject: this comes as a surprise to no one, but i cried again last night

i had some important meetings last night. they all went so well! then i got home and cried for hours because i really, really, really, really wanted to kill myself.

i cried for a very very very very long time. probably hours. i cried because i wanted to kill myself and i didn't know what was stopping me.

i didn't end up killing myself. look at me, here i am, writing this email, alive.

also, i appreciate everyone's concern, suicidal ideation is scary and you wanna help, i get it. but i do this newsletter as a way to track my emotions and as an art project. none of us need to fear crying!!! it's ok to cry!!!! it's ok to want to kill yourself all the time and it doesn't mean you're broken or bad. in fact, you can be functional, like me. (except when you're not functional, like me, last night.)

so for the love of god, stop suggesting i do XYZ to get better. first of all, i didn't ask for your opinion lol. but moreover i have a good therapist and a good psychiatrist and good friends and good family and a ton of support. i have people to go to. i just also write this KOOKY-ass newsletter.

ok should go do real work now.

with love,
eve

$$* * *$$

11/7/16

subject: teared up a tiny bit on Friday, but haven't really been crying

On September 30, the night before my 23rd birthday, I half-assed a suicide attempt. I'm glad i didn't go through with it. the next day, my birthday, i made the decision to quit drinking, at least for the time being. i also began taking zoloft. those two things combined have improved my life drastically. i feel happier, more awake, refreshed, actually excited to be alive!! it's truly beautiful. but the combination of the new meds and the no alcohol means i haven't been able to cry.

so i flourish but my newsletter dies? maybe. who knows what pain stands before me, what will trigger my next bout of uncontrollable weeping. the future is unwritten. but for now, my eyes are dry.

i managed to muster a couple measly tears—a tiny, virtually impotent load—when i was flying from portland, oregon to new york city on friday. they weren't tears of sadness, but tears of longing. i wish i could've cried more, but i'm glad i'm no longer a weeping machine.

until next time,

e

---

* * *

11/10/2016

subject: unsurprisingly, I cried on 11/9

when I woke up the morning of 11/9, I cried a little bit. if it weren't for Zoloft, I imagine I'd still be crying. I'm so afraid for what will happen to women, people of color, Muslims, and LGBTQ folks in this country. I'm concerned for mentally ill people like me, all the people who are silent and terrified and want to die. I'm scared of what happens if I lose my health insurance, if I can't afford my medications. It's a scary fucking time. I'm grateful to have amazing friends and family and mental health professionals in my life.
Stay safe.

Fight the white supremacist heteropatriarchy.

Fuck fascism.

Until next time,

e

---

* * *

12/23/2016

subject: why I cried last night

while I was crying last night I begrudgingly said, "oh great. now I have to write a newsletter."

since I returned home from a two-week trip to Oregon earlier this week, I've been feeling very depressed, overwhelmed with this anger—that I have to be alive, that I have to deal with the utter exhaustion of existence, that I have to take a cocktail of pills to be a functional person in this world.

when will being alive get less exhausting? when will I be able to have real fun, to feel joy without pain? when will the self-hatred rest? when will I become less reliant on other people to feel worthy?

I felt mad and indignant about my mental illness because even though things in my life are going well—friends, family, romance, work are all very good right now—that I still have these feelings. circumstance helps depression, but doesn't fix anything. I know this and I've always known this. but it nevertheless felt so deeply unfair that my psychology propels me toward these death-thoughts, this haunting misery.

I ended up FaceTiming with someone I really like for hours and that made me feel a lot better. having support and love is so important, and I'm lucky to have it.

today I feel less bad than yesterday. that's the life of a depressive—things are better now than they were and it will forever be a struggle to remember life is worth living. but it is.

until next time,

e

* * *

12/28/16

subject: do you ever start imagining all the terrible ways your life could play out...

do you ever start imagining all the terrible ways your life could play out and start to tear up? being alive is scary and hard—having depression means it'll always be hard. even though things are better now for me than it has been in the past but it doesn't mean things are easy. so the world keeps turning.
    stay strong.

until next time,
    e

* * *

1/20/17

subject: happy inauguration i cried again

yesterday i found out i won't have health insurance until march and there's nothing i can do to get it before then and cried about it. i cried about it again this morning. also donald trump will officially be president in a matter of minutes. i'm fucking terrified. i'm so fucking terrified.
    until next time,
    e

* * *

1/30/17

subject: cried yesterday and today

unsurprising considering what's going on in the world.

i cried because a lot of the suicidal thoughts i've been working so hard to overcome began flooding back this weekend. my boyfriend, who was visiting me went back home, and i had to go off my zoloft for a bit after i lost my health insurance. i was feeling so scared and afraid for the future and all i could think about was wanting to die so so badly. a video about suicidality popped up in my facebook feed and i lost it because i related.

i wept all morning, and then the zoloft my doctor sent from canada finally arrived, which made me feel infinitely better.

i worry for all the other people who will struggle to get their medication if the ACA is further gutted or repealed. i worry for the muslim immigrants and refugees who have been banned from entering our country. i am worried.

until next time,

e

* * *

2/7/17

subject: i cried again but i swear it's not my fault

over the past week, my depression and anxiety surged, slowly engulfing me—hasn't felt so bad since before i quit drinking. i hate the feeling—severe depression turns you selfish, lazy, and worst of all, it compels you to do nothing but feel bad for yourself.

the narrative goes: why me why do i have to be alive why is being alive so hard for me why am i not dead i wish i was dead if i was dead i wouldn't worry about all this stuff i wouldn't be in all this pain.

though i was barely able to leave my apartment this weekend, today i felt determined to do better than yesterday, to leave the house before the sun went down, to get some work and errands done. no crying, i told myself. i didn't want another day helplessly stuck in the prison of my bed.

my mission to have a better day was, however, wrecked once i realized something can gone awry with my finances. i know i'll ultimately be OK, but the whole ordeal exacerbated the pain and anxiety i had been trying to move past all day. i broke down and wept and probably (definitely) screamed a little.

even though i was "in a state," having a lil breakdown ultimately brought me some feeling of catharsis. even though i've cried a bunch the past week—and will likely continue to cry in the very near future, if history's taught me anything—this cry felt more necessary. some cries, you just ruminate in your pain and your self-pity and eventually you stop but only because you tire yourself out. other cries, better cries, begin with that self-pitying feeling, but the act of crying allows you to release it; in this case, you stop crying because you stop feeling so sad. i'd like to think my cry today was one of those better cries, but i'm still too close to the situation to make an evenhanded assessment.

i also talked to my mom and my best friend, who both really helped me feel better. i know i say this all the time, but i really am forever grateful for all the support i have in my life.

until next time,

e

SARAH M.C.

MORE THAN ANYTHING, I want to help other people around me. Ever since I was young, I've always helped others before helping myself. I was under the impression from a young age that if you give yourself self-love or self-care that you are selfish. This is, unfortunately, the conditioning that we receive at a very early stage in our lives, especially for young girls since we are primed for motherhood at four years old when we get our first doll. We're taught to care for everyone else around us, no matter what the expense.As

I helped my friends through their own parental struggles, but I suppressed mine, keeping my feelings hidden from others. Only when my friends would come over to our home would they really see the tragic Shakespearean drama unfolding. From the outside, our house looked normal. We seemed like the average family living in a beautiful suburb in a small town close to the sandy shores of Lake Michigan. I went to a public school that was rated more like a private school because of the high academic standards. I played some volleyball, and softball in school, but was drawn more towards the arts; creative writing, and ironically, drama. I had kids comment to me that our family was "rich," and tell me they were jealous that they didn't live in our house. That's because they didn't see the hell that was unfolding inside of our Beaver Cleaver home.

The truth was that while I was busy helping the other kids in school with their problems, I had to learn how to live with my mother's alcoholism.

It started when I was about thirteen years old. That's when I found out that I was an aunt. Everyone in our family knew that my brother had a child out of wedlock, but my parents thought it was best not to tell me until they thought I could "handle" it. To this day, I'm not sure why they thought that. My sweet, little niece was nine months old before I got to meet her, and I was so upset with my parents for lying to me. However, I ended up finding out about my niece months before they told me because of the not so subtle hints dropped around the house. It was also about this time that I noticed that my mom started to drink a lot more than usual.

My parents loved a good party and lived a pretty affluent life-style, but after my niece was born, everything shifted in our home. No longer did I look forward to going home after school. Because of this, I would spend much of my time locked upstairs, blaring my music, dancing, or writing poetry or short stories as a form of escapism from the hell that was below me in the living room. I lashed out with teenage rebellion and started to drink and smoke too, although that only enabled her behavior. My mom bought me my first pack of cigarettes at age sixteen, and let me drink as long as I was at home with her. I also learned very quickly that you don't talk about your problems with others because the first thing people have a propensity to do, is to judge you. The only worse thing than being judged was to be pitied.

When I moved out for good at twenty years old, I thought things would be different, but it was so much worse; the drunken phone calls at work, the weekends of her destroying herself, the cornucopias amounts of cigarettes and beer she consumed to fill whatever void in her soul that needed to heal. Yet, I never stopped loving her. I knew whatever inner demons she had, she was working on it in the only way that she knew how to. I never blamed her for her shortcomings. Where she lacked in some areas, she excelled in others. Like every child of an alcoholic, I desperately sought my mother's approval, and let her own self-destruction also consume me. I felt utterly responsible for her and guilty if I didn't pick up that phone call at work. Sometimes, I would just let her sob and speak incoherently while I typed up daily memos. Other times, I would softly yell at her so my co-workers couldn't listen, of what a mess she is. She never remembered our conversations the next day, so there were some nights where I said some pretty awful things to her.

I wanted so badly not be anything like my mother, but instead, I turned into the thing that I feared the most. I started going to parties to purposely get drunk. I was hoping that she would see how pathetic it was and learn something from my behavior. Instead, she tossed it up for her daughter just being a "party girl". There's actually three years of my life that are a complete blur. I would go to work in the morning, get off by eleven o'clock p.m., go get drunk with some friends, then head back to work the next day. I can't tell you how many times I was stupid enough to drive home drunk. I am so lucky that I never killed anyone or myself in those years.

I was reckless, with wild abandonment, and I didn't care. I just wanted my mother to see me. The truth was that she was so self-absorbed in her own narcissism that she never noticed what I did. As long as the appearance of a "normal" family was there, she didn't really care too much about anyone else unless it was convenient for her. Neither of my parents paid much attention to me. My mom was consumed with grief from her own past, and my dad worked eighty hours a week, leaving me to my own devises a lot of times. I slid by with C's and D's in school, and they rarely ever went to school functions or even my parent teacher conferences unless I was about to fail a class.

I started disliking myself at a young age, and after being

bullied for years, I briefly considered the thought of committing suicide at thirteen years old. Luckily, it was only for a minute.

After that minute was over, I began my own form of therapy with photography, writing, poetry, short stories, and painting. The truth was, I had a lot of potentials, but no on to believe in me. I didn't even realize I could believe in myself because no one ever taught me that either.

It's no wonder why I developed General Anxiety Disorder and Depression as a child. My mother (having the stigmatized belief that if a person has a mental illness, it means they're crazy) never thought once about how her drinking behavior would affect me in adulthood. She never once stopped to think that maybe she had a mental illness. Yet, after seeing one of my paintings, she threatened to take me to a psychologist in a not-so-nice tone. As if I should be ashamed to seek help.

Almost two years ago, I finally broke down and saw a doctor because my anxiety was so bad that I had developed IBS / SIBO . It was caused by years of stress on my digestive system—my intestinal lining had started to eat away, causing leaky gut. One day, I noticed fungal lesions breaking out all over my body. That's when the panic attacks began coming frequently and with more fever.

I was desperate to get to the bottom of what was happening to me that I went to my naturopath with a list of symptoms, and for some reason, on the day of my appointment, I added anxiety and depression.

After careful review of my chart, my naturopath said, "You have General Anxiety Disorder." She gave me some herbal supplements and sent me to see another doctor who also diagnosed me with anxiety and depression.

For the first time in my life, it was urged to see a therapist. Regardless of being terrified, I took a leap of faith and sat through my first therapy appointment. That's when the word bipolar was mentioned to me. Immediately, I thought of my mother, and how my sister and I would comment about our mother's mental well-being. For years, we speculated that she was bipolar too. If I had it, chances were good that she did too.

The cruel irony of all of this is that I had to move 5,000 miles away from my mother to start healing our relationship.

My mother continued to drink until three years ago, four months after my Dad passed away. She quit cold turkey. Overnight. When I told her that I was seeing a therapist, she told me that she went to a psychologist once when she turned forty, too. She told me that when she left there, she was so upset with herself because the therapist made her feel inferior. My mother screamed at herself in the car as she was sobbing and trying to pull it together—telling herself she was "stronger than that." She then added, "That's when I picked up my first case of beer."

I will never forget that conversation. I realized that she didn't have any love for herself, so how could she show love for others? If only she had stuck with therapy and gone on medication, she might not have had the need to pick up a case of beer that day.

After listening to her story, I figured out I was only eight years old. I guess she and my dad hid it well from me until I was thirteen.

Today, speaking with my mother, you wouldn't think she was an alcoholic for thirty years. Being the scared child I was—the one who never knew what to expect when she came home from school, I am still mad at her for that. A part of me might always be mad at her.

However, while I may never have the love I so desperately craved as a child, I do have the love of my mother as an adult. For the most part, I have come to understand the reasons why she drank, but that's not forgiveness.

I so wish I had started therapy while I was in high school because today, I sit here and wonder how much different my life would have been had I sought help. I lived in that hell alone, as a thirteen-year-old girl. I wonder if I would have had the courage to go off to college. If maybe, I would have been a social worker or psychologist like I wanted to be when growing up. I wonder if I would have reacted stronger and not have taken it personally when she went on tyrants, calling me "stupid." I try not to live my life in "what-if's" while also avoiding the thought of regret, but now, as an adult, I can see that maybe I could have been a little happier if the stigma of mental illnesses didn't exist and we both got the help we needed. I would have gotten the proper care and would have saved myself mentally and physically.

As an adult now, I realize I have the opportunity to encourage and support others who are going through similar situations. I want to break down that social stigma with whatever means I have, and that starts here: Being open, honest, raw, and real about who I am, as well as *my* story of how mental illness has affected me.

SPARKLLE RAINNE

I HAD JUST TRANSFERRED colleges and moved two states away. It felt like it'd be a comfortable environment, just four hours away from the town I grew up in, but it wouldn't stay that way for long.

The school was a dream come true, as far as administration and student accommodations went. It was awesome, considering the fact that my last college didn't even have a cafeteria. They even had a police station on campus, which I didn't expect to need, but, unfortunately, it came in handy for me later.

Well, actually, it wasn't that much later.

I had been in school for a solid week, but I had met a small group of people in the area prior to school starting. We quickly became friends since they seemed fun, welcoming, laid back, and just a tight-knit circle of people that I felt like I could get close to.

One of the first things I do when I move somewhere is look for friends. Despite living with an anxiety disorder for entire life and enduring sexual, physical, emotional, and verbal abuse as a child, I've always kept the mindset of: "most people are good." Something that I had always wanted, was a tight-knit group of friends. We had been hanging out for about a month and I really felt like we were going to be close.

One of the guys in the group liked me but I had turned him down and asked to keep things platonic, which I thought he respected. He knew that I had been abused as a child and that I am abstinent.

This experience was very recent, so as I write this, I'm having a hard time deciding how much to share because this story builds up to one night–the night he slipped something into my drink.

It was a Saturday night and a few of us were hanging out. The previous Thursday, we had all hung out and things seemed as innocent as they could possibly be.

I blacked out entirely that night and do not remember much. I came to for a clear (yet quick) few seconds while vomiting and screaming for him to get off of me while we were in the back of a car, but then I blacked out again. I do not remember how I got into that car, nor do I remember how I got out of it, but what I do know is that I had bruises and welts on my left side, and when I got picked up by a taxi that night, I was laying on the side of the road. I remember seeing the word "taxi" in a blur, knowing that I needed a ride home, and getting in the taxi. I don't remember how the taxi was hailed. I only know that I was laying on the side of the road when they picked me up because the taxi company told me this via phone call when I was trying to piece together what happened.

I stayed in bed the day after everything happened. I was sick as hell for one thing, but mainly I was just trying to process my thoughts and figure out what to do.

When I went back to school, I told my instructor because I didn't know who else to go to since I was so new to the school and city. He was very kind and helpful; he told me to go to the police station on campus and file a police report, so I did. They brought in a female advocate from the school–she came with us when the police picked up my clothes from that night at my apartment and stayed with me through most of the time I spent at the hospital that day. I'm so thankful for that because I can't imagine going through that process alone.

I was at the hospital for six hours, waiting and being checked over. Before the advocate from my school left, she connected me to an organization that would provide me a cab voucher for the ride home from the hospital. I remember the accompanying nurse saying, "That's a good thing to know about for the next person."

The next person.

I couldn't stop thinking about the next person–who, what, when? Will their predator be someone they know? A stranger? Why does anyone have to go through this? Why did it happen to me?

When I filed the police report, they asked me if I wanted to press charges. I asked what that would entail, and I was told that if I pressed charges, I'd have to face the person who did it in court. I couldn't imagine having to see him again. I didn't want to keep repeating and re-living what happened, so I didn't press charges.

Instead, I dropped out of school and left. I tried to live normally for a few weeks, but the person knew where I lived. It was off campus and I lived alone. On top of that, my apartment wasn't the safest.

I knew that he'd obviously find out I filed a police report, and I was terrified of what might happen when he did. It was the first time that anything really broke through my "most people are good" mentality. It has made me afraid to make new friends. It has made me afraid to get close to anyone. I ended up buying a greyhound ticket and scheduled a job interview in the area my mom lives in. I told myself that if I got the job, I'd leave school. I got the job. I quit school. Now, I'm just taking it one day at a time, trying to figure out how to move forward–how to finish my degree, how to feel safe, where to move, etc.

Never leave your drink out of sight–not even with friends.

I hope to see a world where every survivor gets justice and I hope to see a world where no one feels too helpless and ashamed to move forward for help.

ME VS. MY EATING DISORDER: HOW I REALIZED THAT I WAS SICK AND LEARNED TO DIFFERENTIATE MYSELF FROM MY SICKNESS

SPARKLLE RAINNE

My EATING disorder began when I was only eight years old. It began with bulimia, but my diagnosis has changed multiple times throughout my life–I've been diagnosed with bulimia, anorexia, and EDNOS/OSFED at separate times during the span of my treatment. By the time I was eighteen, I was binging and purging all day, every day. It never ended. I felt like a hopeless case seeing as I had attempted to recover many times at that point.

Since I was so young when it started, I grew up feeling that my eating disorder behaviors were simply a part of me. I didn't know what an eating disorder was, so my eating disorder was just "a thing" that I did. Many people with eating disorders have a comorbid illness, and growing up with a severe anxiety disorder was certainly a cause for me. The first time I made myself throw up, I was because I was overwhelmingly anxious–you know that feeling when you're so nervous you feel like you're going to puke? I lived with that feeling 24/7 because of my anxiety disorder. The first time I purged, I did it to make that feeling go away. Then, I got addicted to it.

Even though I didn't know what an eating disorder was when I was eight years old, I had definitely heard of them by the time I was ten. I was already devouring books about eating disorders like, "The Best Little Girl In The World," but somehow, it didn't resonate with me that I had an eating disorder.

Despite this, living with my eating disorder was hell. I did have enough of an inkling that I was doing something I wasn't supposed to do because I knew that I had to hide it. However, it took me a very long time to recognize it as something that I needed and deserved to get help for. There are two major reasons for this:

1. No one told me that eating disorders can affect people of any size. I identified with the people in the books that I read since I had the same behaviors, but because there was so much stigma around what someone with an eating disorder looks like, I didn't see myself as "skinny enough to be sick." This is a problematic misconception because eating disorders affect people of all shapes, sizes, genders, races, backgrounds, income levels, genders, etc. Eating disorders are mental illnesses that do not discriminate.

2. On a similar note, I didn't feel that I was sick enough because, well...I wasn't dead. This is very common for people with eating disorders. I was in denial–even when the physical repercussions came along, which for me included fainting, thinning hair, blood in my vomit, amenorrhea, broken blood capillaries, weak bones, and more. Again, though, I didn't feel that I was sick enough to be taken seriously because, well...I was alive, and I didn't see myself as thin enough. Most people don't realize how sick they are until they've already done irreversible damage.

Therefore, we need to change how we talk about eating disorders in the media. We need to continue to raise awareness and debunk myths about eating disorders.

I finally recognized that I had a problem and wanted help for it around the time that I was fifteen. Bulimia had turned into anorexia for me at that point, and I became so sick of how much power it had over my life. As a whole, I felt that I had no control over any of my behaviors. I felt like I was possessed by a demon and since I had lived with it for so long, it was very hard for me to differentiate the demon from myself. In order to recover, I had to do just that: differentiate the eating disorder from myself and figure out who I was without it.

Obviously, this isn't a fast process or an easy one, which is why early intervention is so important. The longer you have an eating disorder, the faster lines begin to blur between you and your eating disorder.

For me, there was hardly a line. I grew up with my eating disorder. Unfortunately, the first time I reached out for help on my own, I was paired with a therapist who had no experience with eating disorders. Looking back, I understand that she made a mistake; she should have referred me to a therapist that had experience with my issues. Seeing her made me feel even more hopeless, so I stopped going to my sessions with her and sank deeper into my eating disorder. By the time I was eighteen, my bulimic behaviors had returned full-force, and I was binging and purging 24/7.

I had been in therapy again with a great treatment team for about a year at that point, but obviously, my eating disorder was deep-rooted by that point. When my psychiatrist began looking for an inpatient facility for me, it was oddly enough, my turning point. I realized that I had to recover, and more importantly that I wanted to. It has been a long road with one relapse in between, but I have been on the path to recovery for four years now. Trust me when I say recovery is worth it and everyone with an eating disorder needs and deserves to get help.

I've decided to end this article by listing a couple of resources that I have found helpful during my recovery:

NEDA (nationaleatingdisorders.org) – the official website of The National Eating Disorder Association. Their website offers information about eating disorders, a confidential online screening, contact information for their helpline, and more.

Proud2BMe (proud2bme.org) – an organization that is dedicated to promoting positive body image and encouraging healthy attitudes about food and weight.

DEAR ANXIETY

ALLISON BARNES

Dear Anxiety,

Today, my boyfriend's father, Sonny, would be turning 66 years old. Today, his family is going to one of Sonny's favorite restaurants to celebrate his life. Today, I am staying home in the comfort of my bed, watching YouTube breathing exercise videos. Today, I had to tell my boyfriend I can't make it out of my house because of my anxiety.

Because of you. I hate you, Anxiety.

I feel guilty, embarrassed, disappointed, and scared.

I hate you, Anxiety.

I live every day with one goal: Do not let anxiety win. Never stop living.

Today, you won.

I feel like a loser, a terrible girlfriend, and a weak human. Yet, I am relieved. You won, and I don't have to leave my bed. My comfort space.

I hate you for winning, Anxiety.

Everyone who suffers from anxiety probably knows how to work through your anxiousness and panic attacks while continuing on with life.

Social anxiety? Go to more parties.
Driving anxiety? Drive more. Trigger
Locations? Go often.

Everyone who suffers from anxiety also knows it's not that easy.

You make the easiest things so hard, Anxiety. I hate you so much.

My first panic attack happened seven years ago when I was a junior in college. It was confusing, terrifying, and memorable. I didn't understand what was happening or what was wrong with my body. I thought I was dying. I said my "final goodbyes" to my father as he rushed me to the emergency room. This is the day I was diagnosed with anxiety.

You came into my life, and you haven't left. I hate you, Anxiety.

Anxiety, you have taken over my life.

My constant worry about a possible anxiety attack makes life dark and difficult. Anxiety about having anxiety is a vicious cycle.

I HATE you.

I wish I could say seven years of suffering has taught me how to get control of you, but I have not come close.

At 27, I am now in the process of accepting you, Anxiety, as part of me forever and always. There is a good chance that I will carry you for the rest of my life, and that thought gives me anxiety. I hate you for doing this to me.

Everyone who has this illness suffers in their personal ways. When my anxiety is high, my heart starts to ache and beat super fast. My left arm begins to hurt. Then, I immediately prepare to have a heart attack. I start to lose my breath, and my body goes numb. I keep one hand on my neck at all times so I can feel my pulse. I tell myself everything is okay; it's only anxiety. Then another voice in my head asks, "What if it's not? What if this really is a heart attack?" My anxiety then increases even more. My face turns red, I can't breathe, can't move, and can't speak. It may start out in my head, but anxiety attacks are very real and much more than a thought.

Why are you doing this to me, Anxiety? I hate you.

Most of my anxiety attacks have no concrete antecedent. I have had attacks while driving. I've had them at work. I've had them at concerts. I've had them at restaurants. I've had them from my bed. Sometimes, there is a cause, but more often than not, they just happen, and there's no reason why. It's not fair, and I hate you, Anxiety.

People without anxiety can't fully understand what it's like to live every day on a level of fear and worry, but they can educate themselves and open their minds to acceptance.

Accepting this is a true illness, it's not only in our heads, and we can't get just over it because we are scared. The best thing for anyone to do in the presence of someone having an anxiety attack is to listen. Make no judgment, remain calm, and listen. Keeping in mind, we didn't choose this. Anxiety chose us.

We hate you, Anxiety.

There are medications, therapy, lifestyle changes, and meditation to help us cope with this illness, but I simply haven't found anything that works for me.

What do we do when we can't be cured? Will my mind ever be free? Will this ever stop?

Please go away, Anxiety.

I know that I must accept this and keep living.

Today anxiety won. Today I failed. Tomorrow I will fight again.

I wish you would go away. I hate you more than you'll ever know. Please leave me alone, Anxiety.

Your Servant,

Allie

27 years old from Baltimore

STEVE AUSTIN

WHEN I DIDN'T SHOW up for an out-of-town assignment, my clients were concerned. When they couldn't reach me, they first called my wife, and then the hotel. The police and EMT's found me mid-morning, unconscious. They thought it was a murder scene. Blood-red vomit covered the bed and the floor. It had projected up the wall behind me and coated a massive picture that hung over the bed. Apparently, the pink Benadryl pills, along with the tens of thousands of milligrams of other medication I took, created the effect of blood. By then I had been unconscious for a solid ten hours.

I should have been dead.

Eighteen hours after I blacked out, I woke up in a fog like I've never experienced before. *Where the hell am I? Why is it so cold in here? Wait a second! Am I in the hospital? Shit! I'm still HERE?!? You cannot seriously mean that I am alive! Do you KNOW how much I took??!!?! Oh this is really bad.*

My son's first birthday was the next day. I don't know what his birthday party was like. I was still in ICU, nearly dead. Three days later, the doctors decided my liver wasn't going to fail, and I had regained feeling in my legs so I was released and immediately transferred to the psych ward.

The psych ward. Me—the former worship leader, youth pastor, radio host, blogger, ministry school graduate, father, and husband. The outgoing one. The friendly one. The upbeat one. Me. I was sitting in a wheelchair, headed to the psych ward. I stayed there for five days. I called it the arts and crafts floor: we colored, talked, and rested a lot. I couldn't sleep the first night because it was too quiet. The experience felt pointless, frustrating, humiliating, and so uncomfortable.

It's been over three years since the darkest days of my life and I am still standing. I still have harsh flashbacks at times, and for a while, I couldn't stand black coffee because I remember crushing up those thousands of milligrams of medicine and pouring the powder into the hot mug, stirring it up, and choking it back that night. The smell, the taste, even the thought of black coffee for months after would send me into a full-blown panic attack.

I'm no longer afraid of my demons, though. We all have skeletons in our closets, and as loud as they may scream for our attention, Love's power is greater.

Once I came to the end of myself, I began to find my true self. I am coming out of a lifelong pattern of shame and stepping away from the expectations of performance-based religion. I am learning to be honest with myself and others about my struggles, and I no longer internalize everything.

I have found the Love that is a belonging, a safe place, a fierceness that will not let me go. I have learned to find the beauty in imperfection and revel in it, and I have learned to enjoy silence. I have learned that my family is a gift.

If the eyes are the windows to the soul, my eyes weren't empty that day. They were just forgetful. They had forgotten to look for the joyful things in life.

If I could say anything to someone who's struggling, it's this: life is worth living. It's worth fighting through all the hard times, the dry times, the lean times, and the mean times. Cut through the busyness and bullshit, then figure out what on earth you're doing here and what your reason is for getting out of bed each morning...and do that with all your heart. Be alone, become quiet, and figure out what it is that still makes your heart beat.

I took a mulligan that day. In golf, a mulligan is literally a do-over. It's taking another shot from the point of the foul as if the first mistake never happened. Friday, September 21, 2012, is my Mulligan Day. It's the day I was given a do-over at life.

INSIDE MY HEAD - PART I

ANDREW BUTTERS

THIS IS the one I do not talk about.

I had always thought that invisibility would be the best super power. That was until I was afflicted with an invisible illness, an invisible condition, and an invisible injury. With so many unseen illnesses and afflictions out there, odds are good you are either a sufferer or know someone who is. Odds are also good that those who suffer also suffer from more than one, like I do. All three of these invisible challenges have had a profound impact on my life and have since they first made an appearance. I understand each of them as much as a layperson should be able to, though that was not always the case. With a little help and a little research these obstructions to "normality" were not foreign for long. The learning curve was tackled without too many issues, probably out of necessity, and likely assisted by several medical professionals—and a dash of Google.

Why then, have I always found it so difficult to talk about one of them? They all have quite a bit in common, most notably the impact on my ability to function in a day-to-day setting. Only one was preventable, but even that is a stretch. I can drone on and on about two of them and have been able to since I was first diagnosed, but the one that I have been managing for the longest, the one that really got inside my head, as it were, I still hesitate to mention. A few times a year I will tweet something about it or admit on Facebook that I was [am] a long-time sufferer, but I can count on one hand the number of times I have had an open and honest dialog on the topic.

I never talk about it.

I had my first panic attack at the age of eighteen. I was alone at the time and dismissed it as something food or alcohol related; a bad burrito or too much tequila. Looking back, though, there was no mistaking what it was. The second one came just before my nineteenth birthday. I was at the movies—Groundhog Day— with my girlfriend and had come from a nice dinner out. With about twenty minutes left in the film, the attack hit me, hard. I could not pinpoint the exact cause but in the span of less than a minute I went from laughing and enjoying myself to hanging onto the armrests like my life depended on it. I broke out into a cold sweat and I could hear my heartbeat in my ears. My chest felt like it was collapsing.

Forced to leave the theater with my girlfriend, she wanted to know what was wrong. "I'm just feeling kind of sick," was the only explanation I could offer. To this day, I have not seen the end of the movie. It has been so long since I have seen the movie that I would have to start over from the beginning and even though I have a good handle on my triggers and am largely in control of the anxiety, I am afraid that if I have to watch it again I will be doomed to repeat the attack and get stuck in some sort of anxiety Groundhog Day loop of my own; which is a shame because I really like Bill Murray.

After a trip to the doctor to find out what the hell was happening, I had a little more information but not enough to fully understand what was going on. He told me I had a panic attack. There was no discussion on anxiety, triggers, or any other underlying symptoms. It was basically, "Here are some exercises you can do to help you work through it [breathing (i.e. meditation), and progressive muscle relaxation]. Don't worry, you'll be fine." To his credit, the exercises helped, but it took a long time —more than a decade —for me to be in control enough that I could quash an attack before it took over.

Still, I never talked about it.

When an attack came on, my wife knew to just leave me alone —there was not much she could do anyway—but she still offered to get me water, pillows, anything I might have needed to make me more comfortable, which was, and still is, a pretty short list. When panic took over, I could not be touched or comforted without it getting worse. I needed to remove all my clothes and somehow stay warm. I could not eat or drink anything. I had to assume the fetal position, head above my chest to keep nausea at bay, focus on something innocuous in the room, breathe, and take my pulse. When I was able to move again, I would take something for the nausea that I knew would also knock me out, only to wake up a few hours later, feeling like I had drank myself silly and gotten into a bar fight.

I wouldn't wish a panic attack on my worst enemy. For me, it ranks higher than a migraine or back pain in terms of its ability to incapacitate. It a whole host of tests and medications before my doctor and I found a treatment path that best worked for me. Paxil. When I moved and found a new doctor, she upped my dose after I had a particularly bad episode. While it kept the attacks at bay most of the time, it wasn't without its side effects. Keep in mind that everyone's personal experience with side effects is unique. For me, for this particular medication, it was weight gain. I was once a bean pole, long and skinny, but the drug saw to it that I packed on more than forty pounds.

And yet, I never talked about it.

Another move, another doctor, and several more panic attacks later, I was still medicated. I met someone else on Paxil, and we shared a few conversations about what it was like to be on the drug. Neither of us were particularly thrilled with it but were not sure we had any other choice. Then I moved, again, this time with two small children in tow, which brought us to yet another doctor. This guy was a real asshole and his bedside manner sucked. At best, his conversations were curt and he was lacking in both compassion and empathy. He also was not a fan of prescribing drugs. Which, in of itself was a good thing, but he had one condition for bringing me on as a patient: stop taking Paxil.

Okay... that came with some pretty big caveats, as well. For starters, he informed me that one simply does not stop taking Paxil, especially if you have been on it for long periods of time. He set up a program for me and told me to seek out a Paxil detox support group on the internet. I even sought out a second opinion from another physician to confirm the approach. Side effects can also come into play when stopping some medications, particularly Paxil and others in the same family, so it was important for me to know what I was getting into, or rather, out of.

Fortunately for me, I was on a lower dose, and my transition off the drug went about as smoothly as it could have. It took ninety-nine days to wean myself off, with the worst of the side effects confined to headaches. There were some panic attacks along the way, but part of what made it go so well was the blog I kept about the experience.

Had I finally started talking about it? Sort of. Well, not really.

I was talking about coming off the drug and all the physical and psychological challenges I was facing, but I was not talking about the problem itself. My friends Anxiety and Panic were still there. Mind you, they weren't as prominent or debilitating as they were in years past, but they were still there, lurking. For the years and months since, they have been following me around. I sit and wait, doing what I can to keep them at bay and hoping that when they do pay a visit the impact is not too severe. The good news is I have a toolkit of breathing and meditation exercises to help me and I know my triggers and have a better sense of how to avoid them.

As a result, the attacks are fewer, but I still have not gone twelve months without a panic attack since that first one all those years ago. My record is eleven and my current streak is three, but this time I am aiming to set a new record and whenever that streak comes to an end, I will look at my wife, my kids, my relatives, my coworkers, or my friends and say, "I can't give you anything today. I'm recovering from a panic attack, and I need to rest."

Because it is time I started talking about it.

It is time we all did.

This is the one I don't talk about.

I had always thought that invisibility would be the best super power. That was until I was afflicted with an invisible injury, and another one, and then another one. With so many unseen illnesses and afflictions out there, odds are good you are either a sufferer or know someone who is. Odds are also good that those who suffer also suffer from more than one like I do. All three have a profound impact on my life and have since they first made an appearance. I understand each of them as much as a layperson should be able to though that wasn't always the case. Certainly these obstructions to "normality" were not foreign for long. The learning curve was tackled without too many issues, probably out of necessity, and likely assisted by several medical professionals – and a dash of Google.

Why then, have I always found it so difficult to talk about one of them? They all have quite a bit in common, most notably the impact on my ability to function in a day-to-day setting. Only one was preventable, but even that's a stretch. I can drone on and on about two of them and have been able to since I was first diagnosed, but the one that I've been managing for the longest, the one that really got inside my head, as it were, I still hesitate to mention. A few times a year I'll tweet something about it or admit on Facebook that I was [am] a long-time sufferer, but I can count on one hand the number of times I've had an open and honest dialog on the topic.

I never talk about it.

I had my first panic attack at the age of eighteen. I was alone at the time and dismissed it as something food or alcohol related; a bad burrito or too much Jose Cuervo. The second one came just before my nineteenth birthday. I was at the movies with my girl-friend- Groundhog Day – and had come from a nice dinner out. With about 20 minutes left in the film, it hit me, hard. Forced to leave the theatre my girlfriend wanted to know what was wrong. "I'm just feeling kind of sick," was the only explanation I was willing to offer. To this day, I haven't seen the end of the movie. Even though I have a good handle on my triggers and am in control of my anxiety, I am afraid that the simple memory of it will trigger an attack; which is a shame, because I really like Bill Murray.

After a trip to the doctor to find out what the hell was happen-ing, I had a little more information but not enough to fully under-stand what was going on. He told me I had had a panic attack. There was no discussion on anxiety or triggers or any other under-lying symptoms. It was basically, "Here are some exercises you can do to help you work through it [breathing (i.e. meditation), and progressive muscle relaxation]. Don't worry, you'll be fine." To his credit, the exercises helped, but it took a long time – more than a decade – for me to be in control enough that I can quash an attack before it takes over.

Still, I never talked about it.

My wife knew to just leave me alone when an attack came on – there was not much she could do anyway – but she still offered to get me water, pillows, anything I might have needed to make me more comfortable, which was, and still is, a pretty short list. When panic took over I couldn't be touched or comforted without it getting worse. I needed to remove all my clothes and somehow stay warm. I couldn't eat or drink anything. I had to assume the fetal position, head above my chest to keep nausea at bay, focus on something innocuous in the room, breathe, and take my pulse. When I was able to move again I'd take a Gravol or Dramamine to help me get to sleep and wake up a few hours later feeling like I'd drank myself silly and gotten into a bar fight.

I wouldn't wish a panic attack on my worst enemy. For me, it ranks higher than a migraine or back pain in terms of its ability to incapacitate. It took years and years, and a whole host of tests and medications before a doctor would put me on Paxil for my anxiety. When I moved and found a new doctor she upped my dose after I had a particularly bad episode. While it kept the attacks a bay, most of the time, but it wasn't without its side effects. I was once a bean pole, long and skinny, but the drug saw to it I packed on more than forty pounds.

And yet, I never talked about it.

Another move, another doctor, and several more panic attacks later, I was still medicated. I met someone else on Paxil and we shared a few conversations about what it was like to be on the drug. Neither of us were particularly thrilled with it but weren't sure we had any other choice. Then we moved, again, this time with two small children in tow, which brought us to yet another doctor. This guy was a real asshole. Forget for a minute that I always felt the need to apologize because he was French and was forced to speak English to me, his bedside manner sucked. He also wasn't a fan of prescribing drugs. This in of itself was a good thing, but he had a condition for bringing me on as a patient: stop taking Paxil.

Okay... that came with some pretty big caveats as well. For starters, he informed me that one simply does not stop taking Paxil. You have to wean yourself off it, slowly, over weeks and sometimes even months. He set up a program that was supposed to work and told me to seek out a Paxil detox support group on the internet. The horror stories about detoxing from Paxil are too disturbing to share but suffice it to say there are documented cases of a detox going so poorly that the patients became suicidal.

Fortunately for me, I was on a lower dose, and my transition off the drug went about as smoothly as it could have. It took ninety-nine days to wean myself off, with headaches galore and several panic attacks along the way. I was a right miserable ass the whole time, but part of what made it go so well was the blog I kept along the way.

I finally started talking about it – sort of. Well, not really.

I was talking about coming off the drug and all the physical and psychological challenges I was facing, but I wasn't talking about the problem itself. The anxiety and the panic attacks were still there. Mind you, it wasn't as prominent or debilitating as it was in years past, but it was still there, lurking. For the eight years and ten months since it's been following me around. They say that you're never truly cancer free and that you will always be living with it. Like the victim of physical abuse who knows that another beating is right around the corner, I sit and wait, doing what I can to keep the inevitable onslaught at bay and hoping that when it does hit that it's not too bad.

Maybe the next time I'll only lose three or four hours sleep instead of the whole night, even though experience tells me it won't matter. Maybe the next time it won't feel like I'm dying, even though experience tells me it will. The attacks are fewer now. Maybe the next time will be the last time, even though experience tells me it won't be. I haven't gone twelve months without a panic attack since I was seventeen. I'll be forty-two in a few months. Maybe the next time I'll look at my wife, my kids, my relatives, my coworkers, and my friends and say, 'I can't give you anything today. I'm recovering from a panic attack and I need to rest.'

Maybe it's time I started talking about it.

Maybe it's time we all did.

INSIDE MY HEAD - PART II

ANDREW BUTTERS

I STARTED TAKING yoga almost two years ago. At the end of our 90-minute class, we lie in corpse pose, Shavasana, to cool down. We clear our minds and meditate for 10 minutes. As we wrap-up the end of this moment of calm, our yoga instructor will say, "As you open your eyes, notice the detached feeling. Wiggle your fingers and wiggle your toes." I always know when I've had a good meditation because I am intimately familiar with that "detached feeling".

The first time I felt it I was seventeen years old and I was lying on my back on the ice. I opened my eyes and my eyes tried to catch focus on the trainer kneeling over me. His lips were moving, but everything was quiet. I felt like I was outside of my body. When the fog cleared and the sound returned the trainer was asking me if I could wiggle my fingers and my toes (he was also asking me if I knew my name, where I was, and what day of the week it was).

I played hockey at a high level until I was sixteen years old. All the other kids were getting bigger and stronger and I was just getting taller and skinnier and I couldn't keep up with the demand to perform at an elite level. So, I dropped down to house league and joined the Select team, which is essentially a travelling all-star team. With most of our games played in some sketchy corners of Toronto, let's just say that things were a little less civilized than the rep league I was used to playing in.

That night, somewhere in the bowels of Toronto, I discovered that it's possible to experience a "detached feeling" shortly after someone swings a hockey stick baseball style at your head and connects with full force. This being 1992, once I passed all the tests and could stand up on my own, I was allowed back in the game. I did miss one shift, only due to the fact that the blow to my head had not just knocked me out but also knocked all the screws loose in my helmet and the trainer had to tighten them all.

Concussions: 1, Doctor's Visits: 0

A year later, I was lucky enough to get knocked headfirst into the goalpost. This was back before the nets had those fancy magnets to hold them in place. Instead, there was an eight-inch-long, inch thick steel rod that stuck half into the ice and half into the hollow post, also made of steel. Suffice it to say that the goalpost won that battle and I once again found myself opening my eyes to that "detached feeling" and the trainer kneeling on top of me asking if I knew my name. The new helmet held up nicely and I didn't even miss a shift!

Concussions: 2, Doctor's Visit: 0

A year after that, I was playing in the nether regions of Toronto again—this time against a team that had a "husky" young lad as their not-so-secret weapon. We had some small guys on our team and some of the parents were worried that they would get creamed. As it turns out, the shorter, small guys made out okay and were able to weasel out of the way without taking on too much damage. The gangly orange on a toothpick guy (me), didn't fair so well. I can remember the feeling of my nose coming into contact with my facemask as the three hundred plus pound *Fat Albert* of a hockey player squished my head between his gigantic chest and the glass.

I remained conscious but had a hard time making it back to the bench in a straight line. One of the parents, who may have been a nurse, but at the very least was a concerned parent, came over and checked me out. "How many fingers am I holding up? Andrew! Focus. No, look at my hand. There you go. Look here. How many fingers?"

I shook my head and tried to focus. "I see two of everything." I didn't play the rest of that game.

Concussions: 3, Doctor's Visits: 0

Those were the big ones. In the same three-year time frame, I managed to run head first into a tree while trying to escape the fuzz as they crashed an underage drinking party we had going on. I ran full tilt into a tree branch while running from a couple local jackasses. That resulted in a couple black eyes and a nice gash on the bridge of my nose. Oh, and I can't forget the time I was learning to do my first ever snowboard trick. I pulled off an almost perfect method air, carrying a nice fifteen-foot table top, only to get leaning too far forward and land on my face.

Concussions: 3, Head Traumas: 3, Doctors Visits: 0

Then there was that time back in 2006 that I went snowboarding with a coworker at night. I slipped coming out of a turn and fell straight back, my head bouncing off the hill and springing me back up on my board. Wobbling my way back down, we took to the chalet for a break where I promptly vomited up my hot chocolate.

Concussions: 4, Head Traumas: 3, Doctors Visits: 0

Which brings us to 2011. On a weekend retreat with some old university buddies, we took the boat out for some tubing. The object of the game: get the guy to fall off the tube. I went first. The spotter tells me that I flew a good two boat lengths off the tube before the back of my head smacked into the water. It took them thirty seconds to get to me and by then, I had come to. The last thing I remember before blackness was the feeling of something like a two by four hitting the back of my head. The first thing I remember after being dragged into the boat was that "detached feeling". Oh, and the nausea. And confusion. And how everything hurt from the inside out. My friend Sean drove me the 45 minutes to the hospital.

Concussions: 5, Head Traumas: 3, Doctors Visits: 1

I was off work for three months. My supervisor told me that my performance was sub-par, even six months after the accident. I went to see a chiropractic neurologist–the same type of doctor who worked with Sydney Crosby after his concussions. A year after the accident, the "detached feeling" finally left me. What it left behind was a damaged brain I could no longer trust.

My memory turned to shit but has improved a bit since. If I can get things into my long term memory I'm fine, but my working memory is trash. It's likely due to a combination of copious amounts of alcohol, various herbal abuses, head trauma, and being in the fortunate position of getting older. A friend who is a neuropsychologist told me that I needn't worry about long term illness like chronic traumatic encephalopathy (the dementia-like degenerative disease many football players get) but there's a question that's always in the back of my mind whenever I'm having a mental lapse. What if this feeling of being lost and confused doesn't go away?

As if suffering from anxiety and panic wasn't enough under normal circumstances, I have my doctor saying things like, "Please don't hit your head again. The next hit could kill you". She doesn't say it to terrify me into being ultra-cautious, she says it so I understand the gravity of the situation. The brain is fragile and really doesn't like being smacked around once, let alone repeatedly.

It's been more than four years since that sunny day on the lake. Before then, outside of the concussions and head traumas, I could count on one hand the number of really bad headaches I had experienced. Now? I can't count them on one hand, but certainly I don't need all my toes to add up the number of days I've gone without a headache. Just now I'm coming off one that almost kept me away from work. It lasted more than seventeen hours.

"You look fine to me."

"Your memory seems good."

"You don't look like you're in pain."

Comments I've had to face, having no way to clearly articulate what's going on inside my head every day. So, I talk about it. Unlike the panic and the anxiety, I've talked about it—a lot. Anything to get people to understand, even a little bit, what it's like to have a brain that doesn't work. Why am I so insistent on a particular routine? Because then I don't have to remember. Why do I need white noise or a fan on all the time? Because my ears won't stop ringing. Why do I need to keep my pills in one of those days of the week containers? Because I got tired of standing in the kitchen with the bottle in my hand wondering if I'd taken them or not.

Why do I need the pills in the first place? Because I can't sleep, but that's another story.

INSIDE MY HEAD - PART III

ANDREW BUTTERS

IT WOULD SEEM that I've hit the trifecta of brain damage. First, I told you about the one I don't talk about: anxiety and panic. Then, I told you about the one I talk about all the time: concussions and post-concussion syndrome. Now, I'm going to tell you about the one I'm tired of talking about: insomnia.

Part of the reason I'm tired of talking about it is because, quite simply, I'm tired. So very tired. Every person out there who has lived with a newborn baby knows the feeling. Anyone who has had a bit too much to drink on Sunday night and had to get up for work on Monday morning, knows the feeling. I can say with one hundred percent confidence that everyone on Earth has had at least one bad night's sleep in their lifetime, and they know the feeling.

Think about how you feel after you haven't slept well. Imagine feeling like that for an entire week. I want you to think really carefully. Imagine how you feel after one night of poor sleep then compare it to what you think it might feel like after a week. Really get a feel for how much worse seven days would be compared with one. Now, imagine that instead of a mere seven crappy nights of sleep that you experienced 150 of them–in a row.

One hundred and fifty nights.

Twenty-one weeks.

In.

A.

Row.

Five months straight of feeling tired and cranky and falling asleep on your keyboard at work and waking up with a jolt, only when your computer squawks at you because your face has just written an entire document filled with:

"jjkak;jjkadjkjkkj;akdskkjdf;alkjkladnnbbnosdiods"

That's how long I suffered from insomnia before I went to see my doctor. One of the first questions people ask me when I tell them this is: "Why didn't you go to the doctor sooner?" It's a good question. The only reasonable explanation I have is that you start to behave like a degenerate gambler. Every night you throw your money into the slot machine, pull the handle, and genuinely believe that this time it's going to pay out. Only, it never does. At least, it didn't for me. Sure, once and a while the machine will set off a few bells and whistles and toss you a couple quarters just to give you hope, but in the end, it just takes all your money and leaves you cranky and miserable as you shuffle your way to the nearest ATM.

By far, though, the most common reaction I get is, "Oh man, that sucks. I slept poorly once and it was terrible. Have you tried [insert one of the 8,000,000 remedies the Internet says helps you sleep]?" The first on the list of 8,000,000 remedies is melatonin and my response is always, "Yes, I've tried it, in varying doses and at various times before bed, and no, it didn't work."

Next comes, "Huh. Worked for [me / my cousin / my hairdresser / my co-worker / …]. What about [insert another one of the 7,999,999 remedies remaining]?" With the exception of a few, the answer will be, "Yes, and it didn't work." This usually continues for about three or four possible remedies (the really persistent will rhyme off more if they just absolutely *have* to have the answer) and then ends with, "What do you do? How do you function?"

My internal monologue and my frontal lobe have an epic battle at this point, with my frontal lobe almost always ending up victorious in defeating my internal monologue's raging desire to blurt out something I'll regret saying. People mean well, I genuinely believe that, and appreciate that they care, but I have tried so many things and am so thoroughly frustrated I just don't have the patience to keep going through exchanges like the one I described above.

I'm getting ahead of myself here a bit, though. Let's get back to my doctor. The first thing she did was give me some drugs to just plain knock me the hell out. It was important to get me functioning again before we could start to treat the greater problem. We tried a couple along the way. There was the one that, every morning, greeted me with the awesome taste of metal in my mouth. It was like I was grinding my teeth on metal spoons all night. It also made it so that getting out of bed was nearly impossible. I'd get some sleep, sure, but every morning I'd have to drag my ass out of bed and force myself to shower. It felt like I was really hung over (but without the nausea), and that I was waking up after being drugged. It was a very uncomfortable feeling.

The other drug was only slightly better in that I wouldn't have to struggle to get out of bed and there was no taste of metal in my mouth, but it would, however, drop me like a sack of potatoes twenty minutes after taking, without warning. It wouldn't matter what I was doing either. Twenty minutes would pass and I would fall over (or pass out if I was lying down or tip over if I was sitting). It was something right out of a movie. One second I would be doing whatever it was I was doing and the next I was out cold. Have you ever seen the video of those goats that fall over any time they are startled? Here it is. Now, imagine that 20 minutes after I take this pill, I am one of those goats and you walk into the room and blow one of those big air horns.

At any rate, it got me a few decent nights' sleep, or at least got me enough sleep that I avoided the full-on zombie state at work. Then, my doctor recommended I enroll in a sleep class. Yes, a sleep class. It turns out, the university near my house offers a six-week course on sleeping and sleep hygiene. It was really good, actually. During the last class, we were doing this one exercise and I fell asleep! It turns out that part of my problem was I would have trouble getting to sleep and when I'd wake up in the night–which was a lot–I'd struggle to get back to sleep again. This sleep class really helped with that, but didn't solve the problem of persistent wake ups, so it was off to do a sleep study.

If you've never done a sleep study, you're really missing out. They hook your head and chest up to something like twenty wires and then monitor you while you sleep. As if the discomfort of all the glue, tape, and wires weren't enough, you're in a room that closely resembles the cheapest motel room you can find, and there's a camera mounted on the wall at the foot of the bed. You sleep as best as you can, and a few weeks later you meet with the doctor. As near as I can tell, there are only two possible outcomes from this meeting: 1) you get diagnosed with sleep apnea and they give you a CPAP machine; or 2) you don't have sleep apnea and they prescribe you drugs. As my apnea score was in the normal range, the sleep doctor went with Option 2.

After more than a year on the medication I was functional, but still not getting the sleep I felt I needed. Then, I got a concussion. That solved everything! I was instantly sleeping for fourteen or more hours a day. Unfortunately, my head healed (or at least established a new normal), and the sleeping problems persisted. I could go on and on with various things I've tried ("chocolate" flavored pumpkin seed flour was the most interesting – and actually worked for a while, but then my body started to adjust and it was less effective).

I'm on Amitriptyline now, just like I was before the concussion, as well as after the sleep study, and I get enough sleep most nights to function. If I get five hours straight without waking up, I feel like I can conquer the world. If I don't, the symptoms are not hard to spot: yawning, forgetfulness, irritability, impaired cognitive abilities, forgetfulness, bags under the eyes, decreased reflex responses...

The symptoms are bad and their impact on a person is as severe as any other illness out there, physical or mental. The problem is that there are 8,000,000 remedies and a person who is at the end of their rope will gladly fork over whatever money they have, and probably a bunch they don't, to finally find The One That Works. I'm just about done trying things. There are a couple of options left to try: One is a mouth guard that keeps my jaw in a certain position to help reduce snoring. Another one is a Kickstarter headband thingy that apparently maps your brainwaves and plays some sort of magic drum beat into your ears. Yep, a magic drum beat headband. This is what it's come to.

I'll close with a quick word of advice to anyone interacting with someone suffering from insomnia. First, try asking the person if they would like to hear some suggestions before actually offering them up. Hold off on the "did-you-try/you-should-try" talk and instead say something like, "That has to be really frustrating for you. I might know of a remedy, just let me know if you want me to share it with you. Is there anything I can do to help your day go more smoothly?" Second, if you see someone sliding on a magic drum beat headband before bed, don't laugh. A hundred and fifty sleepless nights in a row, and that could be you.

ANN ROSELLE

Mania. Depression.

Love. Hate. My children were born, and my heart was full. My family was complete. The dreams of my husband and I were fulfilled. Snuggling with sweet baby smell. The house exuded hope and promise of new life. Nighttime came along with no sleep, confusing rage, tiny voices squalling in hunger and an inexplicably angry mother. One who cried, one who imagined the help was out to steal the children, one who couldn't parent, and one who couldn't love.

For every action, there is an equal and opposite reaction.

In bed, lying still, pillow covering my face, the blinds are closed, the door is shut, and I'm unable to communicate. There is nothing but darkness to envelop me. Going through the motions, giving the bare minimum necessary to survive—medication and therapy designed to lift me and help me escape do nothing. Thoughts of suicide offer relief to a body and mind wracked with pain, and my family is afraid to leave me for fear of what they'll find when they return.

The hospital offers relief, security and a chance to break free of darkness. Initially, I refused help, and attempted suicide didn't help.

We have a breakthrough when I finally hear the words "It's not your fault." I accept the help in hopes of returning to my family: my husband and three sweet boys.

ECT jolts the blackness away, one treatment at a time. I return home with optimism, energy, and ready to engage with life.

For every action, there is an equal and opposite reaction.

I take my medication, and I participate in therapy. My mood goes up and up and up and up. I socialize more frequently because I am now the life of the party. I join the gym to maintain the steady weight loss since the depression lifted. I stop sleeping because sleep is for the weak. I stop eating because I am a life force that doesn't require frivolous things, such as food. I max credit cards, I betray my family, I argue with everyone...because no one has intelligence on the same plane as me. I am a woman, empowered and emboldened to live an extraordinary life. The mortals I am forced to suffer with daily are holding me back. My therapist tells me I am surly, difficult, and incapable of being helped. I am released from care, left to fend for myself.

I attempted suicide for the second time, trying to escape the mess I caused. I make suicidal gestures and then attempted a third time in the ensuing months.

Three more hospitalizations in a total of six months occurred. We finally hear the term "bipolar disorder" and get a definitive diagnosis. We realize I have been sick, very sick. I was sick for a very long time.

Down, and then up. Up, then down. For every action, there is an equal and opposite reaction.

Hospitalizations are followed by intensive outpatient support, which is followed by support groups that are followed by a weekly routine, then biweekly, and monthly care visits. When a person realizes wellness is an option, then life is, indeed, an option.

For every action, there is an equal and opposite reaction.

Trusts were broken, and confidences lost. The aftershocks

rumbled deep through the ground we were left standing on. In the settling dust, days of therapy, in the medication now taken faithfully, and in the leveling moods, I slowly learned to be reliable—to speak the truth, to show up, and to share how I feel. To accept that others have valid feelings is to know I will be okay.

For every action, there is an equal and opposite reaction.

I write. I speak out. I educate. I use my voice now where others cannot or feel they cannot. It is the only tool we have in order to show others what has happened to our brains and that we are fine, and that our disease is manageable. For the one terrible action that occurred in our brain, betraying us with a chemical imbalance, and becoming disordered, there is an equally amazing and opposite reaction in the journey to maintain equilibrium and good health.

Mania. Depression. Illness. Wellness. Sickness. Health.

I am a wife, mother, friend, confidante, nurse practitioner, writer, and teacher. I am wise, kind, honest, compassionate, beautiful, smart and loving.

Mania. Depression.

For every action, there is an equal and opposite reaction.

From my depths of despair and disdain, there is hope, love and bravery.

ANONYMOUS

IT'S ME, ISN'T IT?

MY DREAM WAS to get a PhD. in Philosophy from either Vanderbilt or Princeton. I'd been accepted to both of their graduate / postgraduate programs. It was Spring. I had spent all my years since college saving and planning for this.

My problems started out with a (relatively) simple emotional issue: dealing with a breakup. I was diagnosed with mild depression and prescribed an antidepressant.

Then I took a bad fall playing pickup basketball and landed on my head.

I started having seizures, and the doctors couldn't get them to stop. I was diagnosed with epilepsy.

Everything else in my body started to go haywire. My immune system was killing off healthy cells, platelets, collagen, the lining around my lungs and heart. I was diagnosed with lupus.

I spent a year in and out of hospitals while they tried to figure out how to keep my own body from killing me. I destroyed my back during a seizure and had to have back surgery. My spleen had to be removed, as it was the offending part of my immune system.

When I got out of the hospital, I was in many ways a totally different person. I had lost 80 pounds when I was ill. Then I was placed on steroids, and I gained 130 pounds.

I would go days without sleeping, then sleep for days.

I was diagnosed as being severely bipolar. I tried commit suicide, twice. The first time, I tried to jump out of a sixth-floor window but one of my co-workers tackled me. After that I checked myself into a mental hospital.

The second time I tried to end my life, I took two bottles of sleeping pills, but my best friend, whom I wasn't even aware was in town, came by to see me. Thankfully, he had a key to my place.

I woke up in a small locked room with charcoal smeared all over my face. I had to have my stomach pumped to remove the sleeping pills.

I was in and out of that same mental institution for 9 months. I was in the hospital a total of 18 months over a 25 month period.

I lost all of the money I had been saving for graduate school .

I had been working a federal government job, so luckily it was still there when I got out of the hospital. The people I worked with were very understanding for the most part. They had done everything they could to help me along the way. I felt embarrassed, ashamed and defective in every way.

I was crazy and weak. I had to take medication for seizures and my bipolar condition so I couldn't drink alcoholic beverages.

I decided to play the piano for a dinner theater to meet some new people. I met a girl there and told her my story.

I fell in love with her and we got married. Six years later, she left me and only then told me the truth: she married me because she felt sorry for me.

By that time, I had left that job for a new career in a new town, one where nobody knew me. I swore to myself I wouldn't tell my story to anyone. No one would know. I would just tell people that I met that I didn't drink.

After my ex-wife left, I had a seizure at work and I had to come clean and tell my boss about my situation. This job was different. I worked in a field where I could help people who had been through what I'd been through; being sick and losing everything. I poured myself into the job with everything I had.

With my ex-wife gone, I had a child completely depending on me. When signs of mental illness started to show up in him, I was in denial. I had lived with it myself for years so what was I afraid of?

The stigma wasn't coming at me, it was coming from me.

As time went by, I had become "successful". I had a responsible job at a well-known, prestigious company. I was making more money than I ever dreamed possible. I met another woman with three daughters. We fell in love and got married. I told her the truth right from the start. I didn't hide anything from her. She knew everything, but still loved my son and I. I loved her and her daughters back.

My ex-wife, who felt sorry for me because of my condition, spotted in my son what I had missed. She got professional help for him. He went through a period where things worsened. He was in and out of hospitals for drug and alcohol rehabilitation as well as for treatment of bipolar and borderline personality disorder.

I can admit to people that I have a physical condition. I'm considered an epileptic, as I still am prone to seizures without medication. But why am I ashamed to admit that I'm bipolar?

The answer is that I'm afraid I could lose my job or that my position would be phased out.

I have written several reasonably popular blogs online over the years. I don't use my real name. I'm afraid I could lose everything I've worked so hard for.

I am submitting this article to Stigma Fighters because I want people to know that mental illness is just like any other illness. Nobody asks for it and it's nothing to be ashamed of.

Still, I don't want to use my real name. I've been living a good life. I have people who love me and I'm in charge of making lucrative decisions at work. I'm afraid upper management would remove me if they knew the truth.

Bu then again, I don't think they would. The company has an enlightened policy on such things now.

The stigma is coming from within myself.

It's me... isn't it?

ASHLEY WILSON

Depression wants to take my life. It wants to keep me in the corner, away from everyone so that it can feed me lies about myself and others. I can't honestly say that I try to get rid of depression because it steals my motivation and will to live. In return, I humbly submit to it. Living with depression is like living with a creepy shadow. Everywhere I go, it follows me with its daunting presence and its dark cloud. It rains insults and judgments in my head. It produces guilt, unhealthy suspicion of others, poor self image, anxiety, social awkwardness, and delusions about how other people see me.

Depression is forceful, in that it does not ask for permission to wreak havoc on or in my life. It forces me to isolate myself due to a distorted way of thinking; "you're no good, no one loves you, why are you still even alive, you are a burden." As much as I would like to challenge those distorted thoughts, they are constantly being hard-wired into my brain. They come with agonizing inner pain and sorrow. Depression is dangerous when it accomplishes its goal to be the only voice that you heed to.

I get away at times. However, the depression has an invisible cord attached to me. It will not let me get too far away from it.

When it senses that that I am getting better on my meds it somehow sneaks in to tell me that I am fine, that nothing is wrong with me and I do not need medication. After much thought and much persuasion from this insidious disease, I listen to it and go off of my medication. Then, it tells me, "see you don't need it you're fine."

The depression appears as a light in the darkness that it created. Once I listen and let my guard down it has full access. It pounces, sucking all of my energy, causing me to be unmotivated, telling me that I am nothing and that people hate me. Eventually it shows itself and how it succeeded in deceiving me.

Oh, how I loath depression. It is the friend that befriends me against my will, the energy that thrives on sucking my energy, the culprit that caused me to lose my will to live. The ugly inner beast.

OPEN LETTER TO SOCIETY

CATHERINE STONE

DEAR SOCIETY,

People who suffer from mental illness are not second-class citizens. They are not jokes, they are not puns, they are not attention-seekers. Their lives are not worth any less than your own and their illnesses are no different from those you call 'physical'. It's as if the brain is not an organ as much as the heart, lungs and stomach are. But you, as if oblivious to this fact, look down on these people and exclude them; you are scared of them, you mistreat them, you humiliate them. And I wonder why. Why do you degrade them? Why do you bash them? Why won't you listen to them?

To quote Shakespeare, are they not "fed with the same food, hurt with the same weapons, subject to the same diseases, healed by the same means, warmed and cooled by the same winter and summer" as you are? "If you prick [them], do [they] not bleed? If you tickle [them], do [they] not laugh? If you poison [them], do [they] not die?"

Allow me to pose a question here: have you ever heard of Heinrich Himmler? Along with Adolf Hitler, he was the one who plotted to systematically murder eleven million innocent, human beings just because they were different, JUST FOR BEING WHO

THEY WERE. Well, guess what. The infamous author of the "Final Solution" to the "Jewish Question" was not 'crazy'. A psychopath? In all likelihood, yes. But he was not mentally ill. And all those people... The architects who designed the concentration camps, the builders who made them a reality, the officials who ensured these inhumane places kept functioning as 'effectively' as they did, the members of the disgusting, morally, corrupt Nazi, Party, the masses upon masses who took to the streets either to listen to their beloved Führer give his public speeches or to call for the annihilation of gypsies and homosexuals and Jews alike, among several other minorities — were all these individuals mentally ill? We are talking massive numbers here, so many of them probably were. But all of them? Even a majority of them? No, and perhaps that is the most terrifying part of it all: that these tens of millions of 'sane' people, when put together, were responsible for one of the most terrible moral catastrophes the world has ever known.

To this I would like to add that the criminals you read about in the papers or see on the news — the murderers, the rapists; most of them are not 'crazy'. Most of them do not suffer from any form of mental illness whatsoever.

So, I suppose it is because of all of the above, that I wonder why people seem to be pre-conditioned to believe that they should be afraid of the mentally ill, *just for being mentally ill*, while at the same time, knowing what the mentally sane are capable of.

I know I am writing in extreme terms here and the truth is that some mentally ill patients are dangerous to others. We all know that. But there seems to be a general belief that this small part of the mentally ill population is in fact a majority. Sometimes, writing in extreme terms is the only way to help readers understand just how wrong misconceptions such as this one can be.

You can be bad and suffer from mental illness, but suffering from mental illness does not make you bad. In fact, the stigma associated with these illnesses that pushes so many victims to stay silent out of FEAR until it is too late, is in fact food for their illnesses. It helps the illnesses grow inside of them. If people just spoke openly about mental health, if schizophrenia and mood disorders were taught in schools along with the mechanics of tumors and how to test for breast cancer, if they were taught the signs and symptoms of mental illness from a young age, THOUSANDS of mentally ill children and teenagers could live without shame. THOUSANDS of hospitalizations would not have to take place. THOUSANDS of potential SUICIDES could be avoided. It is not just about acknowledgement or about being kinder or more empathic. It's about saving lives.

Awareness of mental illnesses and the pain and limits that they bring to their sufferers is everything. And yet our children are taught how to dissect a frog, but not how to potentially prevent eating disorders; our children are taught Advanced Physics, but not the signs and symptoms of Depression. And still today we maintain the idea of 'the crazies', and of them being abnormal, and sometimes —heart-breaking as it may be— even guilty of their suffering.

"Normal" is defined, and tends to be understood as "usual". Yet, according to research, one in five people will suffer from some form of mental illness, disorder or impairment during their lives.

Mentally ill individuals are not 'unusual'. Please, for their sake, and for everyone's sake: stop the stigma. Stop the generalizations. Stop hurting them and potentially hurting yourselves. Anyone can develop a form of mental illness at some point in their lives.

If you won't do it for them, then do it for the people you know. Do it for your family members . Do it for your friends.

For Heaven's sake — do it for yourselves.

Sincerely,
A nineteen-year-old girl

BIPOLAR HOT MESS

CHRISTINA HUFF

AUGUST 24, 2006. Who knew that when I woke up that morning, it would change my life forever.

We all have lots of dates that change our lives. Our birthdays, date of marriage, date of divorce, date of graduation, date of children's births, date of deaths, and the list goes on. Having a mental illness can make it hard to remember exact dates. Symptoms can creep up on you so gradually that it's hard to pinpoint exactly when the illness began. Or, you may have had the symptoms all along and never noticed.

We may recall a time when we started noticing that things were not right, or something felt off. For example, the senior year of high school or after a major life event such as marriage, death or job loss. In my experience with my own mental illness, running mental health blogs/websites and meeting others with mental illnesses, an exact date cannot usually be recalled.

There is one date though that clearly stands out in our minds and that is the day we were DIAGNOSED.

August 24, 2006. That was the day I was diagnosed. On August 23, I had gone to work as usual and sat in my office trying to focus on my paralegal duties. I hadn't been feeling like myself for a while, but ever since high school I had always struggled with depression, so I assumed that it was just another wave of depression that would pass. After work I met up with my boyfriend (whom I was living with at the time) and some friends. My boyfriend and I had an argument and I went home. I went to bed and prepared to wake up and head to work the next morning as usual. When I woke up the next morning I found that my boyfriend had not come home. I wasn't really bothered by that because all I could think about was jumping off the balcony of the 4th floor of our townhome. There were cement and paver bricks below. There was no grass, no net, and nothing soft to break a fall. There was just plain concrete. I stood on that balcony looking over the edge and wanted to die. I didn't care where my boyfriend was. I didn't care that I had to be at work in 2 hours. I didn't care that I had two dogs who had been inside all night and needed to be let out before their bladders burst. I just wanted to jump or fall over the railing. Everything felt different that morning. I woke up and instead of feeling tired from a late night out or upset about the argument (as I normally would be), I just walked around in a weird, zombie-like state. I kept walking outside on the balcony, contemplating my demise. After a few trips out there, I came to the conclusion that something was not right.

I called the ER for one of the hospitals in Chicago. I explained what I was thinking and they asked me if perhaps going to work would take my mind off things and might help. I looked down at myself in my pajamas. I decided that I couldn't even imagine getting dressed for work, let alone getting to the bus stop. I would then take the bus to the train, and the train to the office. There I would spend the next 8 hours in a little office in a downtown high-rise, alone with my thoughts.

The operator transferred me to a suicide hotline. After talking to them with little to no affect, I was told to head to the ER.

August 24, 2006. I got into my car and drove to the ER. I had no idea what was about to happen. I had never been to a hospital for an emotional problem. ER's and hospitals were for people with physical illnesses that needed to be treated or at least that was what I thought.

I walked up to the desk and when they asked what brought me there, I told them the that the woman on the phone told me to come. They asked why and I casually said, "I want to die. I really want to kill myself." Immediately, I was taken into a room where a security guard was standing guard. They took my purse and made me change out of my sweat suit and into a gown. I guess the drawstring on the pants and the zipper on the jacket were potentially harmful. After an hour or maybe it was 4, I was handed a form and asked me to sign it. It was a consent form voluntarily admitting myself to the psych ward. I picked up the pen and signed not realizing what was to come.

I was wheeled through several hallways and a series of locked doors that could only be opened with ID badges.

I finally arrived in the psych ward. I looked around slowly and immediately regretted signing that paper. I put up a fight. This wasn't where I was supposed to be. This isn't what I thought I had signed up for. I really know what signing that form truly meant.

Throughout the whole morning, I never imagined what the result of wanting to jump off my balcony would be. As it turns out, it was the best decision I ever made. I didn't know it at the time and I tried to fight it all the way. I threw tantrums and threatened lawsuits, but it truly was the day that changed my life.

August 24, 2006. The day I was diagnosed with Bipolar II. Finally, there was a name for the way I had been feeling and what I had been thinking. At last, someone else was able to confirm that my thoughts and feelings were not normal or just phases in my life. They were cycles, the cycles of Bipolar II.

As I approach my birthday on Oct 1 and turn 35, I think about how my life would be different if I had not gone to the hospital that day. Would I still be trying to figure out what was wrong with me? Would I still feel like I was wandering aimlessly? Would I be on the medications I am on now and would I still be in the same place? Probably not. I may never have tried writing.

My first attempt at showing the public my writing skills was a mental health blog The first mental health group that I had joined gave me a whole group of people who were dealing with the same issues that I was. They could relate to me and help me. That's when I decided that I wanted to help those that were like me.

Now, here I am, blogging, writing and helping others. It's been 9 years and while many things have happened in between, that date is one I will never forget because that was the day that my life changed. I received a diagnosis and was finally able to get the proper treatment to start living a better life.

CHRISTOPHER TAYLOR

WHEN I WAS three years old, my parents divorced. My mother, suffering from bipolar disorder and not knowing how she could raise a child on her own, attempted suicide. I have vivid memories of her return from the hospital. She was so sedated that she could not even pick me up.

With the dissolution of my parents' marriage began my own struggles with depression and anxiety. Years of fighting between my mother and father ensued. At the age of 13, I spent three months in the custody of my father before being sent back to live in a small trailer with my mother. At that time my mother was too ill to provide for or take proper care of me.

We did not have much. There were a lot of men in and out of our lives, many of whom were abusive. I missed 70 days of the 6th grade and was only allowed to move on to the 7th grade after much protest, but I did not last long. My anxiety became all consuming, and my mother, under the pretense of homeschooling me, withdrew me from school. Of course, she never made much of an effort to educate me and I fell through the proverbial cracks. Only now have I found the compassion to forgive her. She has an illness just as I do.

At the age of 17, I lived for a few months in a domestic abuse shelter with my mother in Kentucky. That came about as a result of her meeting a man online and her asking me to move in with them. When we eventually returned to our hometown in Georgia, I decided that it was time for me to earn a GED, which I did with ease—despite not taking any classes. I subsequently took the SAT and was accepted to college. By this time my panic disorder had become so severe that I could hardly leave home at all. I dropped out of college soon after.

I have since been diagnosed with PTSD, ADHD, OCD, major depression, general anxiety disorder, panic disorder, and bipolar type II. However, the two diagnoses that all of the doctors I have seen seem to agree on, are major depression and panic disorder.

I spent the majority of my twenties as an utter recluse. I would only leave home, on average, once every month or so. During that time, I was alive but I was certainly not living. By the age of 25, I decided to pull myself off the high dosages of Vyvanse and Klonopin. Those medications had sent me into a hellish, protracted withdrawal. It took nearly three years for me to completely recover. At that point, I promptly went on a drinking binge which further shocked the receptors in my brain. I thought I would surely die. However, at 28, I pulled myself through and matriculated at a local college. It was there that I met an incredibly wonderful professor who remains my mentor to this day.

Today, at the ripe old age of 30, I am one semester away from finishing my first degree with a 4.0 GPA. I have been awarded two scholarships and I work part time at my college as a paid intern. Even though literature is my passion and I have taken several literature courses, I have decided to pursue a B.S. degree in communications and focus on production media. I am also about to move into my own home for the first time in my life.

I will not say that any part of my life has been easy. I have not had many friends and I have never been in a romantic relationship, although I hold onto hope that at least the latter will change in time. I cannot lay claim to having the most difficult life either. I have never been without clothing, shelter, or food.

The abuse and neglect I have experienced and witnessed have not made me cynical. I have a lot of love to give and I still believe in the inherent goodness of people. I believe my self-directed learning and life-long love affair with reading truly saved me, and I see a bright future ahead of me.

Perhaps most importantly, I am finally on medications that work to alleviate my depression and anxiety. I consider myself an excellent example of the fact that it is never too late to recover and pursue your dreams.

WHY DO MENTAL ILLNESS AND ADDICTION SEEM TO GO TOGETHER SO OFTEN?

DANIEL MAURER

THE DAY I asked myself how I had traveled so deeply into my depression, when all I wanted was to make it stop, I wore an anti-suicide smock and cried in a basement jail cell in Williston, North Dakota.

I wrote that I *traveled* to that place because depression is a journey. But it's not like other journeys that you make with your family for a vacation to see someplace new. Depression feels like you're on a treadmill, and every step is an effort. The wheels keep turning on the exercise machine beneath you and the belt keeps spinning. A person suffering from clinical depression only takes the next step because life keeps on moving like a treadmill. You feel compelled to keep up, but there is no joy in it.

Before I was arrested, I hated the meds I had been given. They seemed to give me an artificial edge and they turned off my sex drive. So I did what many choose to do; I self-medicated.

Opiates were my drug of choice. They gave me the feeling I remembered from my childhood when my mother took a freshly cleaned blanket from the dryer and placed it around my body. It made me feel warm, safe and complete. But I couldn't always get what I wanted. I turned to alcohol, benzos, pot, anything really.

My condition worsened. I felt myself sinking ever deeper into a bottomless pit, but still trying to keep up with the incessant treadmill of time, of life. I kept drinking and drugging myself. I kept trying to catch up. I needed to feel normal again.

Eventually, I was arrested, first for a DUI when my pickup veered off the road at 2:00 in the morning. The second arrest was for felony trespassing I evidently had decided (several times) during a blackout that it would be a good idea to wander around the countryside and sneak into people's homes. Apparently, I thought I could find prescription drugs in those homes.

Amazingly enough, I did all this as an ordained pastor in the ELCA (Progressive Lutheran Church). I was good at what I did and I thought I liked my job. I genuinely cared about people and could preach a good message. However, I didn't take care of myself. More accurately, I chose to self-medicate with drugs that only magnified my depression.

Why did I keeping doing this to myself? Why do others who suffer from other forms of mental illness also choose to do this?

* * *

Current research suggests that up to 5.2 million adults that are diagnosed with mental illness, may also be dealing with the substance-use disorder. Of this number, only half will receive treatment for substance misuse or professional care for their mental health.

Mental illness and substance abuse seem to go hand in hand, like honey and jam on toast.

To add insult to injury, the misuse of both licit and illicit substances often manage to land people into the criminal justice system, which in many cases is broken. People with schizophrenia, especially, find that they not only don't get the care they deserve but also have their worst fears realized in prison!

I was one of the lucky ones. When I was arrested, I happened to have decent health insurance. I not only got the treatment I needed to deal with the addictions but also connected with very knowledgeable doctors who treated my depression at the same time.

The reasons why I gravitated toward drugs and alcohol are complex. The simplest explanation is that while I was using them, the drugs made me feel better. This is a concept that healthy people don't understand. They just can't comprehend why I would keep doing something that was so obviously harming me. They don't understand that one or two hours "OFF" the never-ending treadmill was worth it to me . . . even if it meant misery was sure to follow.

People with other disorders use drugs for different reasons: some use to deaden a past traumatic experience; others use drugs to enhance a certain feeling they want to obtain. There are additional scientific reasons behind this as well—overlapping, genetic vulnerabilities being one of them.

* * *

As I mentioned, I was fortunate. I got the care I needed and deserved. I can't tell you how many others I've reached out to and talked with who said that it wasn't that way for them. The number of people is more than I can count on two hands.

For them, the cycle continues. One man, I'll call Steve, contacted me to be his AA sponsor. Steve had a classic case of depression, and his disease was reinforced with an inability to act. The frustration that I experienced while working with him was such that I knew he needed real medical care beyond the fellowship that the program had to offer.

His options were limited. In my home state of Minnesota, there are places where he could have gone to get the help he needed, but it required an effort on his part too. When you have depression, an effort is a rarity.

One day I left a message on his cell phone. I told him I wanted to meet with him again to see what we could do to get him some medication to address his depression. He didn't return my call. I called again and again.

I drove over to the sober house where he was living only to find out that he had been kicked out. This guy didn't have two nickels to rub together and I knew he couldn't have gone far. I drove around downtown to see if he set up shop in a shelter I knew he had been staying at one before I met him. There was no information.

I called a relative living in northern Minnesota. She told me she hadn't heard from him. I finally gave up and tried to put him out of my mind.

Two months later, the relative I had called earlier messaged me that Steve had been found, dead. Authorities think that he fell after a seizure, possibly from alcohol withdrawal. He cracked his head on the pavement and bled to death.

Steve deserved better than that. We all deserve better than we often get. My view is that the stigma surrounding both mental illness, and the chemically induced variety that so often accompanies the other, have structured health-care to view the issue as a problem of that person's own making.

* * *

Today I live in hope. It begins with sharing our stories, standing tall, and not being ashamed of what we have. Our stories are not yet finished and others need to hear that transformation is possible. Advocacy is key.

I have transformed my life because of the care I've received. Today, I'm a freelance writer with two books to my name and I have made it my life's goal to share my story, as well as others' stories of change. I'm a father, a husband, and a friend. I still struggle, but I know I never need to return to the place I went to as long as I continue to reach out in gratitude.

HONEY

ELIZABETH LEVINE

I couldn't comprehend how Spring would bring new life when my heart was still buried in last September, decaying with the memories of you. But, Spring has came and went and Autumn reigns again, bursting with colorful displays that remind us all that there is beauty in the breakdown of life and in letting go. Like the dance of the last honey bee enticing the Queen before Winter sets in. There is a beautiful evolution in the midst of a dance, between the grandiose ideals of two manic lovers transforming into a loving bond. They discover the renewal of friendship, where compassion and understanding balance chaotically impassioned hearts.

I ran inside from the outdoors in my sundress. My skin was piercing through delicate folds of sheer fabric, draped 'round my breasts. It didn't phase me because you and your family had me in such a whirlwind of excitement, that I had no time to keep my wits about me. My mind was buzzing and there was something new and magical about this Bipolar episode. It was a mania-fueled love affair we were breeding together because up until then, I had always danced alone.

Running inside barefoot, my cheeks flushed and blushed, I skidded into the sunroom where we had made love the night before to Rumi and candlelight. Soothing smoke from the hookah had billowed a delicate veil around us.

You and your father sat in the overstuffed armchair, surprised by my comedic entrance. Hair in knots and draping down my back, breasts on high alert and breathless, I waved hello with a smile.

I interrupted your conversation abruptly as you both stopped short and looked at me like two deer in headlights. We had just finished gathering honey from the beekeeper's hives, where I finally got a glimpse of the Queen. Fitting, as your father took another look at me and boldly said, "She's Queen Material." You smiled and bashfully looked at me with bright eyes, "She sure is. Thanks for doing everything … perfectly."

I sighed while running off, pretending not to hear a word because if I acknowledged what was said, it would have spoiled the perfect moment that was suspended in the air like the dust that was drifting through the cascading sunlight. If only your father knew the reality that was us; a raw expression of residual pain from grief and heartbreak of lovers past.

With any new and profound change, there is always a dose of pain intermixed with fear. The slap across my face was a brazen display of sexual frustration and anger. It was stiff and intensely raw. Shattered wine glasses with shards scattered across the floors. Knives were pulled from drawers and wrestling ensued as you balanced apples on my head, just for the thrill. There were food fights and furiously wicked words spit through the air. Intensity rose to a fever pitch as hidden rage boiled over and time ran wild between what now became a brother and sister gnashing teeth. We consciously decided not to let past pain pollute the present. Forgiveness broke the chains, setting desire and passion into motion under the blood-red moon as it cast dancing shadows across our bare, honey-drenched skin.

That evening, as we sipped coffee under the stars and spoke of the intense shift in this shared emotional space, you gently grasped my neck, pulling my forehead to yours so our eyes had no place to wander but deep within our own. I realized what we had in that moment, was perfect just as it was. There was no striving or desperation to sustain the intensity of flickering and fickle flames. We held onto that moment as we remembered where we had been and our end goal; to grow in love in all ways, either separate or as one.

You reminded me that nothing was guaranteed or permanent in the evolution of love except for the fleeting moment of reciprocal love itself.

After our separation and successful attempts to right our wayward ships, we returned to each other as mirrors. We were masterfully repaired through the healing of time and through the beauty of letting go of what was, while succumbing to what is; love in its purest form.

"Love has come to rule and transform. Stay awake, my heart, stay awake." ~ RUMI If you're one of the lucky ones, you've encountered a soul who is willing to work through the chaotic, sticky process of unfolding and unraveling through the wakening of self or if you have been lucky enough to meet someone who is transforming at the same speed, mirroring the beauty within you as if it were pure magic. Whether lovers or friends, separated or not, through thick and thin, fire and ice, dirty or clean – you're weathering the storm, awakened.

I was one of the lucky ones.

Our friendship is familiar, yet enticingly new. I speak to him in cautious tones, because I know it'll take but a moment to fall back in. I have a profoundly compassionate heart for our journeys because we shared experiences and tripped over awakened states many couldn't understand. I'm wildly inspired because I see him becoming the best version of himself, ever-evolving through the chaotic beauty impregnating this Universe. I test the manic waters because he challenges me with sticky, honeyed-love that saturates his core. It was always this way, like amber-colored royal jelly soaked in pheromones ... stuck on him – a drone bee, once fit to be King.

* * *

I smell honey on your skin,
I hear echoes in your knees;
The shaking and the knocking ...
Honey's the best of these.

* * *

I feel blood dripping from your bones;
I taste the dew of daylight
Waking the fields of gold.

* * *

I sense the wonder of your eyes
and wander in your lips;
I hear the whispers of delight
As your top hat in nature tips.

* * *

I wrestle the nests in your hair
and the knots in your toes;
The sensation of triumph
As the only one who knows ...

* * *

The last dance of the honey bee

Mirrored before the Queen in his understated grace,
As Winter sets in and honey drips from residual heat,
preserved in this unfamiliar space.

ERICA ROBERTS

"Give it up for adoption," he said, waving his hands as he spoke. "I'm sure there are options other than traumatic surgery if you don't want a child." He grinned and sipped his coffee. "But really," he continued, carelessly setting down the cup and nearly knocking it over, "I have zero say in the matter, and so do the pro-lifers lurking outside of Planned Parenthood."

I stopped fidgeting with the rubber band that was tightly wound around my fingers and looked him square in the eye. "I had an abortion because I knew I wouldn't survive the pregnancy."

It's the only time I've ever seen him speechless.

* * *

Nearly two years ago, I fled the Southeast, escaping a spouse that I still have nightmares about. I left with nothing but my car, my clothes, and my cat. It had taken four years of isolation, psychological abuse and two suicide attempts to convince me that it was time to go.

Most of you know that story. But I rarely discuss what happened afterwards.

About five months after I left my husband, I felt like I was getting my life back, little by little. I had a full time (minimum wage) job and was planning on moving in with a couple of people who seemed pretty great. I was finally making friends, and I had been casually dating a guy who, although wasn't right for me, meant well. Day by day, I was learning who I was and rejoicing in having my own life given back to me.

I didn't have health insurance, and so, could not get medication for the depression and anxiety I still battled with on a daily basis. Minimum wage meant I could barely afford rent and groceries for myself and my cat.

A funny thing happens when you've tried to take your own life in the past: you know exactly how many lemons life can hand you before you stare longingly into the abyss.

I knew something was wrong when I was having severe depression episodes – the days where I couldn't get out of bed and felt like grabbing the nearest bottle of pills so I could consume every last one. There were days that I found myself crying at work, with concerned managers hovering over me. I was probably six weeks along when I called my then-boyfriend, my hand shaking as I looked at the little stick with two pink lines. "I'm pregnant," I blurted out as soon as he answered the phone. "I can't keep it."

A couple of weeks later, I sat in the waiting room of a hospital in Vancouver, BC, having elected to go to Canada mostly because it was cheaper than going to Planned Parenthood without insurance.

The surgery itself was painful and trying to get back to my boyfriend's house was kind of a trip: I stumbled down the street to his car, and got something akin to the drunken "spins" as he clenched my hand and drove me to his house.

Once I became fully awake, I felt relieved. Yes, I had sacrificed a few cells. Yes, I had terminated a potential child, and that is assuming that my imbalanced body would have even allowed me to carry the pregnancy to term, but I had saved my life for the second time in less than a year.

And for that, I will not be made to feel shame.

* * *

Abortion is still a controversial subject, and not many resources are out there for women who have gone through it or are considering it. If you need someone to talk to, by all means get in touch with me.

I wholeheartedly believe one can never own too many books, October is the best month, thunderstorms are the best weather, and tea is better than coffee. If I were a dog, I'd be German Shepherd, but more likely, I'd be cat. My life is ruled by my passion for animals, travel, matters of the heart and mind, and creativity. My writing follows suit.

WILL I EVER GET TO WHERE I'M GOING

ERICA SCHWARTZ

WILL I ever get to where I'm going? If I do, will I know when I'm there? If the wind blew me in the right direction, would I even care? I would.

"How did I get here?" It's a question I used to obsess about and feel distraught over. What I felt were the world's standards for my age versus what I had actually accomplished at that point in my life. I grieved over how much I felt had been stolen from me because of my mental illness. I wondered if I could achieve my heart's desires, or if I'd missed my chance. Seventeen years into my journey with mental illness and I feel like I'm on the path to what I'm truly meant to do in life.

I began my journey with mental illness at around the age of fourteen. My grandma recently told me that she has a vivid memory of when she first noticed something wasn't quite right. She, along with my grandpa, were telling my family and I that they were moving half-way across the country. In the midst of the conversation, she realized that I had zoned out. I was staring off into space. It seemed that I was not present in the moment, so much so that I didn't even acknowledge her when she called me by name.

The suicidal ideations also began around that same time. I had intensely, violent thoughts about how to end my life. I was incredibly moody, with highly fluctuating emotions throughout the day. I struggled to deal with life's daily problems. It was originally assumed that my "issues" were strictly hormonal, so I was placed on birth control pills by my primary doctor. The hope was to bring my body back into balance. Little did we all know that my mental instability was much, much worse than just being out of sinc hormonally.

I had my first in-patient hospital stay during the last week of my junior year of high school. It wasn't until then that it was determined that I had severe, clinical depression. I was placed on anti-depressants, and thus began my years' long path of seeing therapists and psychiatrists, working to get on the right treatment plan. I would be stable for a while and was committed to therapy. Then when the regular ebbs and flows of life set me on a downward spiral emotionally, my treatment plan would be reevaluated.

The emotional instability continued throughout college. I had low self-esteem and was not sure of my place in the world. I wondered if I would ever be able to get my act together enough to be able to graduate.

Miraculously, I did graduate college, but I was so disappointed in myself that it took me five years instead of four. My family was proud of me and told me that I should be proud, too. They told me to be proud of what I had overcome to push through and finish college, and proud that I obtained a degree that would open doors for me.

My long-standing, unrealistic standards for myself, and perfectionistic tendencies, highlighted the extra year it took for me to graduate. I had a hard time feeling overly proud.

Post-college life continued to be a struggle. I wasn't getting jobs that allowed me to be self-sufficient. I was an excellent worker and was constantly proving myself, but I always felt that I fell short.

My relationships with the people closest to me in life were unstable. I was hostile towards my parents, I was incredibly clingy to any guy I dated, and was continually desperate to find a group of friends where I felt that I fit in.

My second and third hospital stays were in the Fall of 2008. I had given up hope that life would get better. I was twenty-four, recently lost my job due to health issues, and the foreseeable future looked grim.

Due to my despair, I planned the date and method I would use to end my life. I don't even remember how it happened, but my then therapist somehow got me to confess that I planned to commit suicide while my parents were on vacation. I was immediately sent to the hospital and had back-to-back in-patient stays until I was deemed stabile enough to be released.

I started to feel a bit more hopeful during the winter of 2009 when my psychiatrist and I made the determination together that my long-standing emotional instability was actually Bipolar II, instead of Major Depressive Disorder. Life started to make a bit more sense. My impulsive behaviors, intense mood shifts, and severe depression all fit within the scope of this new diagnosis. With medication changes and continued therapy, I remained stable for several years. I developed very close friendships with a consistent group of people, maintained a solid work history and had a serious boyfriend.

My hopes for the future started spiraling downward after a major life-change in 2014 had failed to work out. It was supposed to be my big break. It was supposed to move me in the right direction, toward my dreams of helping others. It would have given me financially independence, while working with those in my inner circle. When things fell apart, I questioned my choices and my ability to handle significant life changes. I didn't know if I could ever be emotionally stable.

I eventually found hope again. I landed a new job working for a company with a vision that I believed in. I made some great new friends, and began to feel confident in my identity and my ability to accomplish all my dreams. I felt stable emotionally and was enjoying life. I looked forward to what God had planned for me.

I stopped taking my meds cold-turkey and once again, all that I had gained was lost in the blink of an eye. I had my fourth and fifth in-patient stays in May and July of this year. My diagnosis was changed yet again. It was determined that I have Borderline Personality Disorder and Major Depressive Disorder.

The last seventeen years of my life made more sense now and I felt incredible hope when I learned about Dialectical Behavior Therapy (DBT) during my hospital stay in May. I have participated in weekly group and individual therapy, learning practical tools to help me accept and manage my emotions. It's helped me to develop stable and healthy relationships. Between the DBT and a new medication combination, I'm finally getting what I have needed all along.

The wind of life is now blowing me in the right direction I'm spreading the message of my journey, my struggles and victories with mental illness. I'm fighting to break down the stigma associated with mental illness.

Fellow warriors: it is worth it for you to make the investment in your recovery and in your dreams for the future. It's a day-by-day process, but I truly believe that by sharing our experiences, battling together, and believing in hope, we will all get to where we want to be!

PART OF ME

ERICA REVA

"Normal is illusion. What is normal for the spider is chaos for the fly."

— MORTICIA ADDAMS

My life as a liar began when I was very young. I was an awful child. I was constantly making everyone angry. I did horrible things every day. I was clumsy, awkward, and terrible. Jesus was disappointed in my behavior, so I had to be punished.

My parents hated me and my mother's, mother tortured me. I disappointed everyone because I couldn't be "normal." What a terrible child I was. If only I could be better. I had to do better. If I would just listen and not be a 'fat, stupid, slob", then I wouldn't be punished. If I could just be better and not a liar with an 'overactive imagination' everything would be better. That's simple. I'll read about how to be better! I'll watch everyone so I'll know how to be 'good' and 'normal'. If I were like the other kids, I wouldn't have to worry.

I stopped feeling. When being a 'good' & 'happy' child didn't work, I gave up. A heavy veil of nothingness took over, comforting and protecting me. I no longer felt anything. I began working obsessively studying other children. I grew, I learned and I hid.

I stopped being a happy child. I no longer existed. I was gone and would not be able to find myself until my late twenties. Sure, there are a few things I remember. There are glimpses of my old life; a moment here and there, but it doesn't feel real. It's like a foggy dream. It's a moment of happiness that doesn't exist. Just as I stopped existing, so did my memories.

I longed for that moment of happiness but could never feel it. Laughter and happiness weren't safe. Speaking wasn't safe. Sadness, joy, anger, and fear, were not safe.

Nothingness is where I resided. I lived in an empty hole and was covered by nothingness. Nothingness was my security blanket. There was no joy, no pain, and no fear. In a strange way, it was comforting.

Studying the nonverbal languages of expression and the body became my obsession. Later in life, I even began studying it at a college level. People needed to know what I did not understand. It consumed some of them. They began living my life. I had no idea what was happening and to this day I am still missing years of my life.

"Blacking Out" became the norm. I had no idea what was happening to me. Depression and anxiety took over my life. I had moments of wanting to know what was happening. I saw many doctors but none of them could tell me anything. It was the constant, shrug and "I don't know."

I quickly began seeing the signs upon entering a doctor's office. I (we) could always tell if they would be able to help us. None were able. They ran their tests and everything came back normal. Something was clearly wrong, but despite our efforts nothing was being done. I gave up.

In my mid-twenties, I quit. I had no desire to know what was wrong with me. I couldn't take it. My parts, however, were quite different. One refused my defeat and continued seeking help. She would "take over" (meaning I was not in control) and she continued making doctor's appointments.

Eventually, my mother wanted to help me. It was shocking since she was one of the causes of my problems. This threw us into a tailspin. She helped B (the very determined part of me who sought help) get an appointment with the Mayo Clinic. We saw nearly every specialist that was available to us.

The five to seven-day stay was extended to nearly two weeks. My (our) neurologist saw it. He saw them. He 'tested' what he thought he saw, and very quickly realized that he was correct and that we needed help. He saw them. He paid attention. He listened to me which was something no one else had ever done. Not one doctor listened to me or them. If not for this doctor I (we) would not have made it this far. We would have ended our life.

Once we were home, the doctor gave us a long list of follow up appointments. One was to an endocrinologist in Chicago. Another was to a mental health clinic in Indiana. The doctor at the clinic quite literally saved our lives. There was no explanation given for this referral. The doctor just wanted us to see someone else. This new doctor ended our guilt over many things, and she continues helping us today. She helped B find her voice. She has helped Anger be so much more than she was... She showed us we could live. She wasn't afraid, regardless of what they had said or done in her presence. She listened. No one had ever done that before and it was truly invaluable.

We continue seeing this doctor to this day. For now, it's twice a week, but it won't always be. Living with DID is a struggle, but having an actual support system now, something we never thought we would have, has helped us continue to grow. We found our voice. We found it acceptable to reach out to demand support and respect. We've learned to ask and hope. Hope was lost to me and most of us for nearly twenty-eight years. Hope would creep in briefly and then be locked away. Now, we Hope. We speak to my husband about these things. My best friend now knows about our struggle. She knows about "The We in Me."

We found our version of normal. We no longer live like a fly, but as the spider. Never dilute yourself to please others. Never silence your own voice because someone says you're "Crazy" or not good enough. Create your own path and live. We did.

FREE

ERIN KHAR

THE FIRST TIME I thought about killing myself, I was seven or eight years old. My parents had recently separated. With their separation, the thin film that had kept me from falling into a dark hole wore through. In fact, I had recurring dreams about it, about a hole, in our front yard, sucking me in. No one would see me disappear. That hole held all the feelings and it set my brain on fire.

Part of what I just said might be a lie, not about the hole, but about the first time I thought about killing myself. I was not seven or eight years old. I was younger.

I had trouble sleeping from about the age of four. It was around the time that I was sexually abused by an adolescent boy, who was a friend of the family. I don't remember the sequence of events, because my memory pushes them together in an accordion that folds and unfolds involuntarily. But, I do know that when I couldn't sleep, I would keep my body as still as possible, holding my breath, counting the seconds, wondering if I could hold it so long that it would stop- me from breathing.

The first time I felt any real relief from the threat of that black hole, the one that followed me around pulling and tugging at my feet, was when I stole an expired Darvocet which was an opiate from my mother's medicine cabinet. My mother didn't take them. They were left over from one of my grandma's hospital stays. I didn't know what it was, but it was large and red and beckoned to me from the bathroom shelf. It worked. I didn't kill myself that night and the hole got smaller. I could still see it, but it couldn't touch me.

Over the next few years, any time I felt that darkness nipping at my heels, I'd steal a pill. I became gifted at sneaking a Valium or Vicodin, or two, from medicine cabinets whenever I used someone's bathroom.

As I approached my thirteenth birthday, I felt increasingly stifled by that black hole of depression. My father was distant, both literally and figuratively, and my mother, while loving, was embroiled in the soap opera of her personal life. Then, I tried heroin.

I was thirteen and my boyfriend was sixteen. He offered it to me and I didn't hesitate. To the outside world, I was doing just fine. Actually, I was better than fine. I was popular, I got good grades in school, and I was involved with horseback riding, cheer-leading and volleyball. But, I did heroin on the weekends and stole pills. Then I started cutting myself.

Throughout my teenage years and into my early twenties, I used heroin off and on, I cut myself off and on and I stole pills. I hid that layer beneath my skin, the layer that held all the secrets, shame and fear. I hid it from nearly everyone around me, including friends, boyfriends, parents, and therapists. That pulse of depression became so strong at times that I literally had to sit on my hands to prevent myself from giving in and killing myself. I would literally dig my nails deeply into the backs of my thighs until I bled.

My heroin use escalated sharply by the time I was twenty-three. I got caught, and went to my first rehab. The focus became the addiction. I relished it. It was a relief and I knew I wasn't crazy! I was a drug addict. I had felt so ashamed for so long about using, but then when it was out in the open, it gave me a reprieve from the other thoughts, the bigger thoughts that kept me up at night, that kept me running in all directions. No one knew what was really wrong, that I was crazy.

For five years, I went through a cycle of relapsing until I got to a point so low that I stood on the roof of a building. I was strung out on heroin and had been up for days smoking crack. I watched the city beneath me, knowing that I had to decide if I wanted to live or die. I wasn't sure, but I knew something had to stop. A feather-weight difference in the right direction led me to reach out for help.

I went back to rehab. It was during this second trip to rehab that I first began to realize and admit that the drugs were a symptom. The real problem was my brain.

That was the turning point and the beginning of getting well, but it has taken years for me to get to where I am today. Even after having my son, functioning well as a mother and off of drugs for almost a decade, I found myself across a table from the man who would become my husband. I had been acting out in destructive ways, sabotaging the good relationship we had. He laid it all on the line and told me that he loved me and that he wanted this to work, but that I needed to get help. I needed to address my mental health issues or we were through. I heard him.

I went back to therapy and got back on medication that I should have stayed on before. My life began to fall into place. FINALLY, after more than thirty years of holding my breath, counting and wondering if I could make it all stop, I faced that black hole that lingered at my feet.

Sometimes I spy the black hole, from the corner of my eye, but instead of running, I stop and wave. I talk about it, write about it and I'm honest about my struggles with depression and about the years I spent using drugs to try and "fix it." I have no shame. I never thought I would be able to say that. Sure, there are things I look back on that I'm not proud of, but I no longer hate myself for any of the mistakes I made along the way to becoming who I am today. Because of that, I am free.

EVAN MORGENSTERN

I REALIZED something was different when I was in grade school.

When I was six, the compulsions were small – like scratching my nose exactly five times or touching part of my bedpost before I went to sleep. But as I grew, so did they. Even though we were not a religious Jewish family, I would pray every night worried that my prayers wouldn't count if they were interrupted. If I was interrupted, I thought I'd have to start over so I didn't incur God's wrath. Once, when I was 9, I peed myself during prayer. I was afraid to tell my dad about the accident and embarrassed by the thoughts I knew I couldn't explain. When I finally told my dad all he said, "When you have to go, go!"

Part of the difficulty of being a child with OCD is that adults often chock up odd behavior to "kids being kids." Adults misdiagnose or may not be truly aware of the true nature of the problem..

In my teens, OCD started affecting my social life. Part of my OCD included germaphobia and, as my high school years predated the use of hand sanitizer, I had a hard time. The bathrooms in my 4000-student-high-school were atrocious and I spent long periods of time wiping down toilet seats with little packets of tissues I brought for the occasion. When I finished, I often washed my hands until they bled. I hoped teachers would be ok with my time out of class and that other students wouldn't assume I had severe stomach issues. Regularly getting upper respiratory infections (all that hand washing...) and having constant sore throats that kept me – an already shy kid – quiet didn't help either. Avoiding getting sick became a painful challenge.

After high school, I wanted to try to have the "true college experience" and live in a double dorm room. My roommate, however, did not make this easy. He began selling drugs from our room, including LSD, which I had had a fear of since the scary PSAs of the 80s and a teacher who comically worked "bad trip" warning stories into every subject. The idea of accidentally touching an acid-laced surface in our room and having a bad trip consumed me. When I woke to see him at the foot of my bed one morning, drunkenly peeing on my stuff, I decided it was time for me to go. It was all single units after that.

After a year of medicating myself to sleep with full doses of NyQuil, I realized I needed a change. Obsessive thoughts kept me up at night. I worried repeatedly that a person would break into my apartment with a baby, stick my dirty fingers in the baby's mouth, and cause the baby to get sick and die. I checked my car more than 12 times one night. I couldn't stop thinking that it wasn't parked exactly within the lines and a woman would have to park further away. She would have to walk through the dark, and then be attacked.

I dropped out of classes and when I was down to only one hour of a sleep a night, I decided to start cognitive therapy with an LCSW. It went well, at least for a while. I felt uncomfortable telling her all my habits. I was reluctant to take medication because I felt uninformed about it and worried it would remove whatever introverted personality I had left to offer.

I put medical treatment off at first, but now I realize it's necessary and no one should be ashamed. While I think that no amount of therapy or medication will cure me, I believe I have the right to see medical professionals that will work to find out what the best course of treatment for me is.

I WILL CRY IF I WANT TO

HENRIETTA M ROSS

I sit, hunched, with my knees pulled up to my chest. It's just the
sofa, the old standard lamp, and me. I am hiding behind the couch.
"Breathe."
They can't see me. The sofa, with its old gold tassels shrouds me
from the window. I wish I could draw the curtains. The doorbell
rings. They thought the chime they had chosen was soft and
melodic but it isn't and never has been.
Rocking, back and forth, I build momentum. I can rock myself
right out of here.
The doorbell rings again.

"Please Stop."
I am on the bridge of a power plant and evacuation is in process.
The warning system blasts like a siren inserted into my brain. I feel
sick. My head is heavy. I feel like I am going to topple over.
"Breathe."
The lights flash like lightning bolts. My limbic system feels as if it
has caught fire. Heavy footsteps trample my neurons. My brain
shakes and spins on its axis and vibrates in my skull.
"Breathe."

It was made of glass. The glass had just blown out. The door was rattling. Could a person outside slip through the letterbox? Is that even possible?

"Breathe."

The doorbell rings again. Someone's finger must be stuck. They will destroy me with an innocent tune. What do they want?

"Please go away." "Go away." "Go away."

I WANT TO SCREAM.

"Breathe."

Don't scream, they will know you're here.

"Breathe."

"Breathe."

The doorbell keeps ringing. My chest is tight. My arm is numb. I can't breathe. I can't breathe. This must be what a heart attack feels like. "Call an ambulance." I can't. I can't leave the sofa. This is the only safe place. Don't take it away. Don't soil it by death.

They're gone. I think they heard me.

My back is pressed tight against the door of the cupboard behind me. My brain is on the floor. Shards of glass glisten in the light. Can I turn the light off? How do you put a brain back together again? Humpty Dumpty never managed it. No one teaches you how to reconstruct one's mind when it has crashed.

From behind the sofa, I creep into the kitchen. The blinds are open. Could the person come through the front gate, walk around to the back of the house and Peer through the window?

It's had bird shit on it for weeks. Can't be bothered to help clean it. That Starling knows the world has turned to shit. We have a symbiotic relationship, the birds, and I. I should put on a drama in the garden, invite everyone, and create a stage out of cardboard boxes. I could rig up some lights and cook some sausage rolls. What do I have in my cupboard? There is some beetroot. I don't eat beetroot so why do have ten jars? Who bought ten jars of vile pickled beetroot?

A memory floods my brain. It still works. I rub my head, and whisper thank you. I bought the jars. It was for a party, a party for one.

I went to the supermarket for party food and bought a whole array of snacks I didn't like. She tried to throw it all out. She put it all into a black bag, walked out to the dustbin with a frown, and muttered something. They don't understand.

My party was killed by black plastic and a woman with a perm. It was completely offensive behavior to ruin someone's fun just because your cupboard is tight for space.

"You can't keep buying this stuff." You bought ten copies of the same book last week. I said I needed ten copies. I did. People don't understand the pressure. It's pressure in the brain. Do as you're told. Buy. Buy. BUY.

Maybe a book in party bag would be a good idea. Forget a yoyo and a party popper. Forget cake and a mini box of Smarties. A book on the First World War would be nice.

"Where are the books?" They were stacked up here. Now there is just a pile of clothes with shirts like Pat Butcher wears in Eastenders. Where did they come from?

"Breathe."

I am dressed like Pat Butcher. "Is this a good look?" Have I been out? Did someone fall over because they were laughing so hard?

I cried. I cried about people not understanding fashion and innovation. I cried about people not understanding creativity, color and form. My head had been in someone's lap. Whose lap though? Which lap? Where?

There were gaps in my memory, days lost, weeks lost with no recall. Space and time were exploding like an asteroid in my brain. There was no linear dimension to give assistance to the filing system. It was like memory banks minus the glue. There was nothing to use as a hook to remember one's life.

Bipolar Affective Disorder. That's what it is called. Beetroot, parties and WW1 in your cupboard. Odd clothes and birds taking a shit.

Windows and breath that come in gulps. Numb arms and tight chests. Blown brains and shards of glass. Sirens and lights. Warnings.

I can hear it. I can hear the doorbell. It's ringing again. The person has come back. This one is persistent.

"Go away." "Go away." "GO AWAY."

"Oh, actually, do you want to come to a party?"

HEYDON HENSLEY

Depression is two hands, squeezing and strangling you until you're dry, so dry that you wonder if desiccation only happens to corpses.

Depression is the fear that you're immortal in a world of goodnight kisses painfully laced with cyanide. You are staring into the void and letting it seep in until you are all that is left. You are a walking silence punctuated by pain that is never revealed. You shout silence into the world and others may hear the currents, a sort of love calling for them to wreak havoc against you again.

ILANA MASAD

THERE IS no single story for the origin of mental illness. There are genes and the matter that passes through them. There are early onset signs that may be treated if they aren't missed or ignored. There are traumas that bring forth something in the brain's chemistry that wouldn't have come about otherwise, but there is not a single, unifying, explanation for mental illness.

As a logical person, an atheist, a believer in science and technology, you would think this would drive me nuts, but it hasn't. My search for the origin of my eating disorder, depression, and anxiety has long been abandoned. I can tell where some of my more neurotic patterns come from (I over-explain sometimes, like my mother and I am unable to do things half-way even when they're not important, like my father), but I cannot tell the exact moment when I became mentally ill. That's okay because for me, the most important part is having my symptoms treated.

My father died when I was sixteen. My therapist thinks a lot of what I've experienced since then must have something to do with that trauma. He was an amazing father, and I helped take care of him during the eight months of his illness. Those months and his subsequent death made me an adult before my time, and it took years before I felt that people my own age had caught up with me.

Context helps. At least, it does for me. Knowing the sequence of when and how things got started, when they were diagnosed and when I began to feel better about them, helps me see how far I've come. I am a writer, a storyteller, and my mental illnesses don't exist without their own narrative.

I graduated from high school, in Israel (where I spent most of my life) in 2008. I took a gap year to universities and colleges here in the United States. In Israeli high schools, there are no guidance counselors to help you with college applications because few people go on to college right after high school. Israelis complete their mandatory two to three years of military service right after high school.

I was not going into the army. My plan had always been to go to college in the United States where I was born and which I considered just as much my home as Israel.

I worked during my gap year. I researched and applied to eighteen schools. I knew that was a lot of schools but I was convinced I wouldn't be accepted anywhere because, despite my stellar academic record, there were no AP classes in Israel and no extracurricular activities on my record. Having boyfriends, losing one's virginity, starting to drink and smoke, don't count.

I was a bit chubby and somewhat pear shaped back then, though others told me otherwise. During that year, I had a boyfriend I loved. When I started losing weight, he liked it at first. He compared my old body and my new body to two different types of cars he liked; one was a run-of-the-mill car and the second was a Ferrari. He doesn't remember saying this to me. We had been together for two years and were very much in love, and it took me a long time to admit that his words probably sent me into a deeper spiral.

Even before my boyfriend had made that comment to me, I knew what I was doing, or at least I thought I did. I had read a couple novels in which girls had anorexia or bulimia, and even though the message in those books was that it is a terrible, haunting, and hurtful disease, I found it attractive. I admired the self-control which was involved, and when I saw my ribs and collarbone for the first time, I was thrilled.

Work helped, since I had hours at a time when I wasn't around my mother. She did finally notice that something was going on though. She and my boyfriend (who by that time, had grown alarmed by my boniness) helped me realize that I was ill and needed to see a therapist. I'd been accepted to colleges and had chosen which one I wanted to go to but my mother threatened that she wouldn't let me go if I didn't get better. I did get better, sort of.

At college, my boyfriend and I continued a long distance relationship. I had two terrible roommates but loved to study. I buried myself in the library and got straight As in order to avoid my roommates and food. I played Magenta in the Rocky Horror Picture Show shadow cast and felt brave for exposing so much of my body. Looking back, the pictures were scary. I look skeletal in my maid uniform and teased up hair. I had to leave school after my first semester. I spent a year on medical leave. I read one hundred and forty-four books that year. I took a class about Classical Greece. I worked with a therapist and a dietician. I was diagnosed with depression by a psychiatrist and worked with him on finding a medication that made me feel better. When I tried to go off the medication a year and a half later, I made stupid decisions, and had to go back on it. I still hate my body. I don't know if I'll ever stop, but I feed it and nourish it now, by habit as well as out of fear of returning to that place where every breath of wind made me shiver. I always loved the cold, until I got so skinny that the cold scared me. I never want to go back there again. Recently, a new psychiatrist diagnosed me with anxiety. I'm on too many meds for my liking, but I take them anyway. What I've achieved since beginning to get a handle on my eating disorder and depression is too good to give up.

I spent a year at Oxford University and graduated. I started calling myself a writer and then became a working writer. I have been published and I have been (and am) loved by good and beautiful people. I am continuing to work on my "issues." I live with my brain every day; I don't hate it anymore.

I AM NOT A MARTYR

J.C. HANNIGAN

GROWING UP, I was told a lot that I am brave and strong. I was told that I handle my chronic, pain bone disorder, Multiple Osteochondromas with grace. Those I loved were attempting to lift me up, but it had the opposite effect. It suffocated me.

I was afraid that if I showed how truly scared I was of having another surgery, or how sick and tired I was of the pain, that my family and friends would think less of me. I bottled it up inside. I tried not to complain when the pain got to be too much, because I knew my parents were powerless to help me. All they could do was take me to my specialist and schedule another surgery. I didn't want more surgeries.

Surgeries meant that I wouldn't be able to pretend I was healthy. The art of denial was a big part of my life when I was in high school. If I denied my differences, ignored my pain and pretended to be like everyone else (all while hiding each scar and tumor under layers of baggy clothes), then maybe I would fit in. Surgeries made that impossible though, because it meant time away from school, long recoveries, plenty of additional pain and it was much harder for me to hide.

It wasn't just about hiding. The worst thing about surgery, for me, was always the anesthesia. I hated the taste and complete loss of control. I hated the heaviness in my limbs and eyelids. I hated the three second count down, and then waking up hours later in the recovery room even though it felt like only five minutes had passed. My mouth would be as dry as sandpaper and I would be completely disoriented. My heart would pound and I would fight to stay awake because I hated drifting to that place of groggy, unconsciousness. It was a total and complete loss of control.

Even now, after having had over twenty-five surgeries to remove the painful bone growths, panic surges every time I step inside a hospital and smell the scent of disinfectant and medicine that lingers in the hallways.

It has never gotten easier, but I grit my teeth and push through it because I really don't have any other choice.

Society puts the chronically ill on a pedestal. They treat us like martyrs, and are quick to compliment us on our strength and bravery whilst also quick to change the subject whenever we admit just how hard it really is. We are martyrs, but they don't want to hear just how terrible things can get for us. Our chronic pain makes them uncomfortable, and they do not know what to say to us.

But we are not martyrs, I am not a martyr. I am a human being living with a chronic pain bone disorder, and I would feel far more comforted by those around me if they took the time to listen to my stories instead of slapping a hero sticker on me and calling it a day.

WHERE IS THE SUNSHINE? A JOURNEY THROUGH THE STORM INTO THE LIGHT

JEANNIE H.

I DON'T RECALL EXACTLY when it hit me, but it hit, and when it did, I was lost. One-minute I was the epitome of the girl who had everything; successful, with a beautiful family, and a wonderful home. The next, I was in a wild vortex unable to escape. I was jobless, hopeless, and wondering what, if anything, the future had in store. If you're OCD, Bipolar 2, Anxiety-ridden or like me, all the above, you know exactly what I'm talking about; the unrelenting perfectionism, the non-stop workaholic and the need to help everyone and everything around you. There I was, left with nothing but fear and worthlessness. I was stuck in the daunting world of my own rumination.

Losing my job was an epic, devastating turn of events. My so-called "life's purpose" was snatched away in a cold board room by an unfamiliar lawyer who made me feel as valuable as a cardboard box. Sick, scared, and overwhelmed, I ended up in the ER, in my pajamas, because coping with something of this magnitude was just not my forte.

The random police officer who stood guard in the ER, listened intently as I recalled what landed me on a gurney. He suggested I think of the film "Jerry Maguire." Naturally, my brain pulled up

Cuba Gooding, Jr. shouting "Show Me the Money" and the multiple references to my alma mater, Arizona State. In a rare moment of clarity, I understood. None of this is worth it if your life has no meaning other than one thing. In my case, my work became my addiction, my remedy and the cause of my illness.

While staring up at the fluorescent lights from my bed in the hall at the city hospital, I thought about this side project that I had been toying with in my mind. Combining my love of inspirational quotes, education, humor, art, and all-around positivity, I started "Where is the Sunshine?" Why sunshine? It's simple. As a musician and former music educator, I recalled the countless song lyrics meant to motivate; "Sunshine on my shoulder makes me happy," "I can see clearly now the rain is gone," "The sun'll come out tomorrow," "I got a pocket full of sunshine," "I'm gonna soak up the sun," "Here comes the sun" and so on and so on. I realized, for people like us, it's nearly impossible to think the sun will ever return or better yet, the storm will ever end, until it's over. I kept thinking when will MY sun return? Where is this sunshine that everyone keeps talking about? Metaphorically speaking, all I could see were brooding clouds and the tornado that was my life spiraling out of control. I guess you could say my song should have been "Stormy Weather."

I found my sunshine. I found the way for me to heal just by spreading positivity and hope. I have learned more about all types of illnesses like PTSD, eating disorders, schizophrenia, and suicide, but I also learned that spreading happiness across social media can be cathartic.

I've learned even more about the stigma these illnesses face. They are mental illness and they are not the same as a broken leg, diabetes or cancer. People run from mental health disorders. It frightens them for they equate it with danger, sensitivity, fear and instability. The reality is, these illnesses need to be met with love, support, encouragement, and understanding for this is the key to healing. Therapy, medication, exercise, nutrition, and other forms of treatment are also necessary, but your support system is what makes them effective.

Most people face mental illness alone, afraid to tell others. For those who are open, reactions are varied.

The online community is probably the most welcoming place for those with a mental health disorder as the support runs world-wide. Admittedly, the concept of support from strangers is unusual, but I have witnessed strength by the thousands. The irony is that people online tend to say and comment about whatever is on their mind, bad or good. When it comes to battling a mental illness, whether it be depression, postpartum, social anxiety disorder, or suicidal thoughts, the resources and support are there and they really do help.

In my case, the online communities have inspired me to want to go out and share my message with others. Getting involved with the National Alliance on Mental Illness, Active Minds, and similar organizations have given me renewed purpose. I love helping others and inspiring people, but I've learned to practice gratitude, to live in the moment, and appreciate everything I have. Nothing, especially a job, is worth feeling hopeless or worthless. There are other jobs, schools, societies and organizations out there, but there is only one you. I'm glad I found the sunshine.

JENNY HILL

I HAVE TRICHOTILLOMANIA. Trichotillomania (Trich for short; also, known as TTM or hair pulling disorder) is an impulse control disorder characterized by the compulsive urge to pull out one's hair.

I've had Trich ever since I was almost seventeen and in my junior year of high school. I'm not sure why or when it started.

I pulled my eyebrows and eyelashes. Sometimes I'd pull less, other times, more. You may be asking yourself, doesn't it hurt? And the answer is no, it doesn't.

For three years, I didn't know that I had a disorder. I merely thought it was just a bad habit. It wasn't until three years after I started pulling that I saw an article online about an actress that said she pulls her eyelashes out. That's when I first heard of Trichotillomania. Oddly enough, I didn't think any more about it at that time.

This past February, I decided to look into it, because it was getting worse. I googled hair pulling and a Wikipedia page about Trichotillomania was one of the first links that popped up. I clicked on it and read it. After that, I went on YouTube and typed in Trichotillomania. I was curious to see if there were any videos about it. I found several YouTubers who had videos in which they shared their story of Trich. I was so happy that I wasn't the only person that pulls out their hair.

Trich is a very common disorder, yet unheard of because a lot of people feel ashamed and embarrassed about it. I used to feel that way. Research shows that two to four percent of the population has it, which means that one to two people out of every fifty have it. That's a lot of people!!

In April, my Trich became worse than it's ever been. I started pulling hair from my head in addition to my eyebrows and eyelashes, however, I pulled more from my head than the other areas. In fact, I've barely touched my eyebrows and eyelashes, because I'm trying to grow them out.

One thing I have learned along my journey with Trich is that it's a very mysterious and unpredictable disorder. One minute you'll have a huge urge to pull and then the next, you won't. One minute you'll be pulling one hair at a time and the next you are pulling three or six at a time, sometimes more. Quite often, I try to stop myself from pulling, but the tension is so strong that I pull anyway. When I do pull, it releases tension.

There's are times when I will pull every day, several times a day. Then there are times where I pull only a few times a day. There are also times when I'm pull free for a few days. That's when I'm the happiest and I feel on top of the world. That's when I know I am capable of recovery.

Slowly but surely, I've been spreading awareness on social media websites such as Instagram, Twitter, Facebook and YouTube for the past five or six months. I have two videos dedicated to my Trich on YouTube. One is before I started pulling my head hair and the other is an update. My hope is to not only spread awareness for Trich but also other disorders as well as Mental Health in general.

I sincerely hope everyone who has read this has learned at least a little bit more about Trich. Please remember that if you have Trich, you are definitely not alone.

LEARNING TO BE PRESENT

JILL JANKOWSKI

I HAVE LIVED my life by to-do lists ever since I was a child. Throughout high school, college, my career, and my home life, I have meticulously planned out each activity and relish the moment when I can check something off the list and move on to the next. A dwindling to-do list has always been my source of feeling productive, of feeling like I am doing a good job at all the things people expect of me in order to be accepted and labeled as "strong" or "valuable" or "important"—or maybe just "normal." As much as I have grown to love my to-do lists and my constant busyness for more than half my life, it has been a crutch for something much bigger that until recently, I struggled to let most of the world in on: I am constantly fighting with my brain and battling a war of depression, anxiety, panic, and OCD (Obsessive Compulsive Disorder).

I was diagnosed with anxiety and depression for the first time at age fourteen. I went to a private high school where I excelled academically in honors classes. I participated in extra-curricular writing and arts clubs. I did my homework every day right after school. I went out for pizza with my friends and talked on the phone for hours at night. I had posters of my favorite musicians wallpapering my bedroom. On the surface, I was as typical as a teenager can come. But as I said, I had begun the fight with my brain. My brain started to tell me that I wasn't doing enough, I wasn't good enough at the things I was doing, and that I wasn't perfect. My brain would tell me to compulsively hate myself, not accept myself for who I was, and believe that I was isolated even though that couldn't be further from the truth. As a young person, this was very difficult to express to anybody—how could my teenage friends understand what I was feeling when all they cared about was shopping, boys, and which movie we were going to see on Friday? How could my parents take me seriously when they would probably just think I was being dramatic and going through puberty? So, I didn't tell anybody for a while. I just self-harmed and took out my confusion and hurt on my body because that's what felt acceptable and comforting. My brain resisted against going to therapy when my parents finally found out, and resisted coming to terms with any of this for the foreseeable future.

Fast-forward to nineteen years old: My brain had been building up an arsenal of self-hatred in the form of anxious and depressive thoughts for five years. I was in college and I had struggled to figure out what I wanted vs. what I thought was acceptable for a career. I was constantly worrying I wasn't applying myself enough or doing the best I could. I was college-hopping in hopes of finding a school that somehow spoke to me and let me know I was in the right place. I was also growing more critical of myself physically, and beginning to struggle deeply with self-image. A toxic relationship sent me over the edge, and I had to confide in my doctor that I was feeling out of sorts. It was the first time I was put on medication to deal with my brain and this constant fight. I didn't take it seriously, though. I thought it was just another trivial way to numb myself that was more appropriate than alcohol or smoking.

When I found myself in the ER after taking half the bottle in one night, and realizing I had been on the brink of death just an hour prior where my mother found me slumped on my bed, I realized this was a big problem that was not going away. I went to rehab, and there I learned that anxiety and depression disorders are real; legitimate health conditions. They aren't just the result of having "feelings" or being "incapable" of handling what life throws at you. So, I did rehab, I went to therapy, and I was put on less addicting medication. This made the next eight years seemingly pleasant. There were bumps in the road, but I learned to reengage myself with activities, projects, and lists of things to do and plan. I learned to become an expert at suppressing my feelings and almost having none at all. I learned to hide my problems even better than before. I learned to cover up my issues by excelling into my career, settling with a long-term partner, creating a home with pets and nice décor, hosting dinner parties and going out with friends, visiting family and putting my achievements on display during the rise of social media. Like I said, seemingly pleasant, but not authentically satisfying as I would come to find out.

Age twenty-seven really smacked me in the face. I was planning a wedding, and before I knew it, I was walking away from my partner. I wasn't happy, but I didn't want to admit I was part of the problem. I called out the reasons why he made the relationship strained, but I had been suppressing my anxiety and depression for so long that I pretended they weren't there, truly being equally as responsible.

When we separated, I sunk into those familiar feelings and they came back stronger than ever. Pretending feelings don't exist to protect yourself for so many years is like getting hit by an eighteen-wheeler internally when your body finally caves and accepts them again—good or bad. After a brief relapse into severe depression, I reconnected with my long-term partner and made a conscious effort to go to therapy. I committed to it for the first time in my life, and I was able to successfully go through treatment for eighteen months to repair my relationship. That wasn't my only problem, though. My relationship might have been on the mend, but my brain was still winning the fight—my anxiety, depression, and now panic and OCD, were still running the rest of my life.

Fast-forward to now: I am twenty-eight years old and finally able to say I have come to terms with my mental illness. I realize that I have nothing to be ashamed of, and realize that what I go through is very real, and very common. I no longer feel compelled to pretend I am someone else for the majority of my day, then go home and let the demons out to play in the comfort of my solitude and privacy. I face the demons head-on at all hours through multiple forms of holistic treatment and, most importantly, honesty. Everybody in my life now knows what I go through—I have been writing publicly to spread awareness, not only of my suffering, but also of the grip mental illness has on so many others. I have a stronger relationship built with my partner, and his support and strength amazes me every day. My family has been open to the understanding and education needed to support someone with mental illness, and they have been an incredible constant in my journey. I have a workplace that is behind me every step of the way as I handle treatment the right way this time. I have an appropriate care team of professionals that are aiming to guide me towards coping and healing in a way that is empowering and healthy, instead of suppressive and numbing. The only reason this has been made possible is because I have learned to speak up and not be afraid of labels anymore—not to live a double life, not to think there is such a thing as "normal," not to think that I am incapable or weak, and not to think that mental illness defines me.

As much as these positive changes mean to me, there's one more that stands out. Those beloved to-do lists of mine still exist. I still make them every day. I still enjoy planning projects, activities, and events that excite me, allowing my imagination to run into the future at times and perceive it exactly how I want it to be. The most important thing is that these to-do lists are not a crutch anymore, and I don't live my life by them. I make them as a guide, but not as a rule. I am learning to embrace my feelings, wishes, and wants—to live in the present. If the present doesn't dictate what's on the list—so be it. We must all learn to love the present, and be in it fully, even when our brains want us to be elsewhere.

Because it's all we have. Right here and now, I feel free, I feel full, and I feel satisfied with the pace in which my life is moving. I am learning to love myself, and accept myself for what I am right now. It is enough to know that, after fourteen years, I am finally beginning to win the fight.

MY SUICIDE ATTEMPT DOESN'T MAKE ME UNLOVABLE

JORDAN GRAY

WHEN I WAS fourteen years old, I tried to kill myself.

Whether my brain chemistry, raging hormones, a recent breakup, or chronic low self-esteem were to blame, I can't say for certain. Often, depression doesn't seem to need a reason. Like an uninvited house guest, it simply shows up when it wants to.

I swallowed a bottle of extra strength pain killers (that I had been carrying around for a week) and waited for them to take effect.

I had never felt number. Tears moved down my face, but I didn't feel sad. I walked around outside in five-degree weather wearing a t-shirt, but I couldn't feel the goosebumps that I saw on my arms. I felt nothing. I was the same way before I had taken the pills. My depression ravaged every feeling from my body. I couldn't access any of it.

Had it not been for an amazing friend who managed to track me down, I wouldn't be alive to write these words today.

I was admitted to a children's hospital and put on suicide watch for several days.

It felt like prison-life; No belts. No shoe laces. No metal cutlery. For some reason, I was the only child in the unit who wasn't allowed to use metal cutlery, and the other kids looked at me as if I was extra dangerous because of my plastic utensils. I would be lying if I said I didn't feel like a bit of a bad ass for getting special treatment, even in this context.

The worst part was seeing the looks on my parents faces during visiting hours.

Before seeing their faces, I had managed to convince myself that they would be better off without me. Truly, I thought I was doing them a favour when I sat down and started ingesting those pills. In truth, the loss would have affected the course of their entire lives. Every time people asked them how many children they have, a lump would appear in their throats...even decades later.

When they visited me in the hospital, their eyes were already red from crying. They looked more exhausted and in pain than I felt, and I immediately felt guilty. "This is the pain that you cause people," my mind scolded me.

Looking back from today, it's difficult for me to grasp the thought processes that I remember going through.

One of my absolute greatest fears was that, since I was more prone to anxiety and depression than others, I would forever be difficult to love. I worried that I would be a burden to any partner who I managed to lure into my life. More than that, I felt deeply unlovable.

This is how shame works its way into our hearts.

Guilt says we did something bad (i.e. "Your actions caused your parents pain"), whereas shame says that we are inherently bad (as in, "You only bring pain to your parents lives because you are a terrible person").

It has been fifteen years since I tried to take my own life (my first and only attempt). What I've learned since then is that not only are we lovable despite our flaws, darkness, and mental health issues, but we are lovable with those things. Furthermore, we are often the most lovable where we feel we deserve love the least. Our pain and darkness is what deserves love first.

I believe that our relationships (intimate and otherwise) are all brought into our lives for the ultimate purpose of healing.

With the people that we meet and attract, we are shown parts of ourselves that we didn't know existed. Everyone you know acts as a mirror to you and is an opportunity to help you heal something that you have difficulty facing.

Since my suicide attempt, I have had the good fortune of being loved by some of the most incredibly compassionate women that I could have ever dreamt of. And their collective message was the same...

While your darkness doesn't define you, it ultimately makes you shine that much brighter in the world.

Your struggles have made you who you are as a person. The depth of pain that you experience gives you that much more empathy and compassion for others who are in pain.

Every experience you have ever been through has only served to make you grow, to make you more resilient, and to make you more compassionate to the experiences of others. Everything you have been through, whether it was immediately apparent or not, was a gift.

Regardless of any mental health struggle you have experienced in your lifetime, you are still worthy of love and belonging. Nothing will ever change that or take the truth away from you.

If I can leave you with one message that you can strap to your metaphorical shield on your darkest days, it would be this:

You are beautiful, complete, and whole. You are worthy. You are lovable. Always.

KELLEY C.

I KNEW SOMETHING WAS WRONG, even as I sat there shaking from the rage. This wasn't normal. I hadn't been this angry for a while, not enough to shake, feel numb and like I'm about to explode.

My bipolar disorder was rearing its ugly head again.

The slightest things set me off. Often, this sudden onset of rage is directed at my boyfriend. He never deserves it, though. But I'm only faintly aware of this fact. Afterwards, when I'm no longer in Hulk mode and I'm back in Bruce Banner mode, the guilt becomes immense because I have my awareness back. So, I cry because I know I've hurt the person I love and that in those moments of unfiltered rage, I was a pretty terrible human being.

In many ways, my bipolar issues mirror my mother's own issues much too closely. I see myself acting out toward my boyfriend the same way she acted out toward my father. The way I manipulate and use my words to hurt people is the same way she carefully crafted her own hateful, rage-filled speeches to hurt her own children and husband.

I don't want to be her, but at this point, it looks like that's where I'm headed.

Therapy is an "option" for me, and I have access, as well as the means to do so, but right now, I'm too scared to go. In addition to having to spill out my life story in regards to why I suffer from depression and anxiety, I don't know if someone would take a teenager seriously when they say, "I think I have bipolar disorder."

I have lived with my mother for seventeen-and-a-half years, so I know what bipolar disorder looks like. I wouldn't fake it just to get attention because it's a terrible, nasty thing. Those years of wishing I wouldn't turn out like my mother were for nothing since I still turned out to be a monster.

Maybe I'll get better, but maybe I won't. Maybe I'll be stuck by myself to handle this disorder for the rest of my life. No matter what, though, I want to try and get it under control because I'm tired of hurting other people, and I'm tired of being so angry all the time.

SOME PEOPLE JUST SUCK

KEVIN HINES

CAREFULLY MANEUVERING to catch my third flight of the day, I reached the line to board the plane. Dressed in royal blue, the gate agent made his first announcement: "Anyone who needs assistance, extra time, or has a disability may board now."

I approached the front of the line. "Pardon me," I said to the older fella next to me. He wore a bright white tee, black khaki shorts, black socks, and a perplexed look upon his face.

While I was well in ear shot, he aggressively proclaimed, "You're not even dragging a leg...that ain't right!"

Pre-board rules are clear: if you have a disability, or need extra time (like I do), you may board prior to any of the first tier boarding sections. What the gentleman who made these remarks did not know, could not know, was the copious amount of physical pain I was in at that very moment. What he didn't know, was the momentous pain I live in daily. How could he? I don't visibly appear to be in tremendous pain, aside my furrowed brow.

However, it is a cross I must bear for the suicide attempt I made at nineteen years old. I hide it well. As he said, I don't walk with a limp. I take my light pain meds and muster through it. I don't complain about it to anyone besides my better half, nor should I since it's a mostly a private reality. When I fly anywhere, the pain is exacerbated. Let's face it, no airline I know of has ergonomically correct seating. Sometimes I am in so much pain, it brings me to tears. So, I just sit there balling. For those who don't know my physical suffering is rather invisible, this fact does not make it any less of a reality.

I would have loved to put that guy in his place, and all people like him in my shoes for just one flight because my guess is, he wouldn't last five minutes.

The injury to my formerly broken, and shattered back was extensive after my attempt. My lower back was fitted with a great deal of titanium. I am not only blessed to be mobile, but clearly, to be alive, as well.

In the year 2000, while struggling with a mental illness, I leapt off the Golden Gate Bridge to die by suicide. That day, my brain was trying to kill me as I desperately fought to stay above water.

Today, I travel across the United States, and the rest of the globe to speak publicly about my experience. I talk about my survival and my ongoing recovery. I do so as I continue living with chronic pain and suicidal thoughts. But that's ok, because I AM ALIVE!

I get the amazing ability to be a part of this world every single day.

I am not alone in this regular occurrence. People like me come from all over the world. We have what most call disabilities. We are those whose suffering is not apparent, and thus, the constant discrimination ensues. Some call it stigma. Do we call bigotry, racism or sexism stigma? No, we call it by its real name: discrimination and prejudice.

I know how lucky I am; I still have the gift of life. In a moment, it can be taken away. I get to kiss my wife every morning that I am home. I am allowed the opportunities to speak about my brain disease to those who are in need of hearing my story—foundations, hospitals, universities, conferences, law enforcement, high schools, grade-schools, and the military, etc.

There are so many people at airports around the globe who

look on with judgment as I board—from the questioning gate agents and passengers to the flight crew. The passengers especially glare on. They screw their faces at me as I board. Others peer on with nasty stares, and yes, some spit out sly comments.

They do so as if those living like me have just committed some heinous air crime. They are the apathetic, without the ability to hold concern. They are the ones with a sad life, being cynical, judgmental, and angry. I hope this blog opens some of their eyes, but at this very moment, as I key in these words, I cannot continue. The pain is too much to bear, and tears are beginning to flow. You get the point. Love on, live long, and find a modicum wellness because your brain health matters as much as your physical and emotional health. Frankly, both should be considered and treated as one...just health. Keep waging this courageous battle #StigmaFighters. I am right by your side.

I'LL ALWAYS LOVE YOU, BUT I DON'T FORGIVE YOU

RYAN RITCHIE

I BELIEVE THAT, at birth, the bond between us and our parents is the strongest that it'll ever be.

It's one of the only raw and unadulterated moments in our lifetime. Where uncertainty doesn't exist: there are no filters switched on that day. Words aren't needed—our eyes tell it all.

A gentle smile forms on your mother's face, which creates a valley where her tears of joy flow to. Your father adores every breath that you take, allowing him the ability to pace his heart with yours.

Realizing that we are their children, we are also a product of their pain, their love, and their bond. It's at this point, this... insanely powerful moment that we are reminded of how precious life truly is.

Sometimes...I wish I could experience that day one more time —to share a moment of oneness with my family; to feel utterly consumed by their love. My parents' love—the way it's supposed to be.

As a parent, your purpose in life changes the moment your child is born, no matter if it's your first, your third, or your ninth—

you are supposed to love, protect and cherish your child. After all, we are, ultimately pieces of them.

If you're brave enough to bring a person into this world, this, fucked-up, bizarre world—it's your job to provide shelter from all that is bad while we learn to grow-up, and as we find our feet with our first steps and begin to understand that this revolving piece of rock is now our home.

Unfortunately, along the way, this can be forgotten.

The one item on my 'parents' checklist,' which is supposed to be permanently completed, was simply overlooked. At first, not purposely, but as time moved on, I realized that their priorities changed.

They had forgotten to love the piece of them that needed it the most: me.

They replaced goodnight stories with arguments. They started to forget that I was there in the morning. They didn't stop to notice that my eyes were slightly darker than usual and that my smile was less frequent.

Their focus was no longer on me but, instead, on their ever-growing hate for each other.

And, I'd try...I'd try really fucking hard to show them that I still loved them. That I still wanted to care. I wanted to show them that I could still make them smile—even when they made me feel so worthless.

I'm not saying that my parents didn't love me or that they mistreated me. What I'm saying is that they stopped treating themselves with respect, they stopped loving each other; which meant they found it harder to find time to love me.

At night, I could hear them. Every night.

The screams of anger and of regret substituted a kiss on the forehead followed by a gentle 'sweet dreams.' Eventually, the screaming would stop, and when it did, I'd stay awake and cry because I was alone.

There was no longer a night-light to fill the crack in my door to make me feel safe. There was no sound of soft footsteps to check if I was asleep. I felt lost.

The fighting would happen so much that I started to numb the mental torture with physical pain. I started to learn that razors would cut deep enough that it would take all my energy to control the blood so that I didn't focus on my parents' ability to isolate me anymore.

Now that I look back, I have one burning question in my heart: How could you not realize that I was not okay? That I was suffocating in consistent tidal waves formed out of your indifference?

The boy, the child, the person you brought into this world was now exposed to the harm you swore to protect me from.

I deserved more of a chance. You should have given me...more of a chance.

For nearly a decade, you prevented every opportunity that I had of being normal. My outlook on life was poisoned by your inability to act like fucking parents.

You were so focused on killing each other that you failed to realize that it was slowly destroying the boy that you created.

And, even though you forced me to become a different person, I still have a place in my heart for you because that's what children do: they irrationally love their parents.

Despite your mistakes and blatant disregard for anybody who managed to get sucked into your hurricane, I still love you.

I blame you both for the life I have today. I blame you both for making me the strong person that I am, I blame you both for nearly a decade of anxiety. I blame you both for teaching me how not to love someone, I blame you both for showing me how not to be a parent, and I blame you both for teaching me so much about life.

If you ever read this, Mum and Dad—just know that I understand. I know that it was never your intention for me to turn out how I did. But, I hope, deep down, that you're proud of me: of who I've become.

I'll always love you... but I'll never forgive you.

KEVIN NORDSTROM

You WALK into the old basement gymnasium. The silence is only relieved by the crawling ticks of cheap lighting and the desperate whine of a fly that followed you in from the cold. Lucky for you the fly leaves you alone and heads for the tiny snack table that's covered with stale donuts and smells of burnt coffee.

There's no movement as you reach the dimly lit circle of chairs. You move around to the side and pick a chair, the green one, and settle into the smooth, cool plastic.

"I always used to pick the green one, too..."

My voice startles you as I make my way across the room. I walk directly across from you, pause, and then grab the ugly mustard yellow chair from where it sits and switch it for the only other green chair in the room and take my seat.

I look down for a moment, silent. I take a few ragged, nervous breaths that sound like paper being torn to shreds. Finally, I stand up.

"Don't worry," I begin. "There's no one else coming. I figured if I'm going to be comfortable doing this I'll do it best in a setting that's familiar. Hence, the overly clichéd group therapy meeting room."

I go quiet again. But this time it's only for a moment as my hand makes it way to my face, slowly stroking my beard as I collect my thoughts.

"I don't even know where to begin... I'm not a writer, by trade. I'm actually an illustrator. I guess in that case, let me start by drawing you a picture...."

* * *

I'm fifteen years old. I'm on the floor of my room, curled into a ball, like a hand becoming a fist. The corded phone dangles in front of my face, but I can't see it for the tears that cloud my vision before falling in random patterns down my face.

I'd just found out that the first person I'd ever learned to love, Lydia, had been killed on her walk home by a drunk driver. It was a path I'd forced her to walk that night, refusing to let her stay at my home where my mom would discover she'd been all day. I was selfish, and she paid the price.

Alone and lost, I stay on the ground as my world crumbles around me. I feel a chill like I'm stepping into dark, freezing waters that slowly makes its way up my body to my ribs, stopping my breath.

I feel like a grub growing all wrong in a cocoon, and I imagine this must be what going mad feels like.

But I'm not mad.

Not yet.

I'm angry.

* * *

What happened next, happened quickly. I fell into a bad crowd, feeding the dark seed that had been planted in my soul, allowing it to grow and flourish. I hurt people. It wasn't fair that so many others got to love and laugh together while I was left to suffer alone. I kept my rage and pain a secret from those closest to me, and it fueled me on my quest to punish others through violence and manipulation. Those years seemed weird, revved up like the strip teasing mannequins and quick change furniture from The Time Machine.

This is where my paranoia was born. I gave fake names, lied about where I lived and kept the good-kid mask on when I was home. My illness hadn't sprouted yet, but it had begun to seep into the folds in my brain like oil.

Soon enough, this life caught up to me and the moment I'd always silently prayed for was coming. I was going to die. I was going to see Lydia again.

But there was a problem. I couldn't remember what she looked like.

I was horrified with myself. Like Sweeney Todd, my rage had become more potent than the love that first kindled it.

And then, by fate or happenstance, I survived my brush with death. But I was left with overwhelming guilt and pain that wouldn't subside.

What would Lydia think of all I've done? Of what I've become?

My mind had become lost in a storm, like Dorothy being swept up in a tornado.

And, sure enough, when I landed, I wasn't in Kansas anymore.

* * *

The final layers of my old self were shed, and new ones took their place. My lust for vengeance was replaced with an obsession for justice and redemption. My paranoia in full swing, hiding everything from everyone. I was on a mission.

I was convinced I was special and that I wasn't an emotionally scarred young man, addicted to an endless cycle of self-annihilating violence. After all, stranger things have happened.

And I wasn't alone, a man who'd once worked for the FBI but was now a private investigator had been watching me and knew my potential. He wanted to help me. It worked out so perfectly it HAD to be fate.

This went on longer than it should have. But no one knew what was going on. I didn't let anyone in close enough. Until two people, a close friend and a new girlfriend started to dig through the walls I'd set in place so many years ago—walls that were meant to protect me but ended up becoming my cage.

The truth began to break through my stories like the light from bullet holes on a western wall at sunset. They confronted me, but I stood my ground, adamant that they didn't know what they were talking about. But each excuse that fell from lips dissolved like sugar in coffee. The cops and gangbangers who always followed me were absent, my private investigator ally wasn't real, the notes I'd receive were missing…

The Wizard of OZ had been exposed, and all I was left with was a sad, lonely man behind a stained curtain.

* * *

I spent an evening in the local psych ward for evaluation. It was terrifying. I can't imagine a place like that being conducive to anyone's mental health. The doctor said I was a Paranoid Schizophrenic. I agreed to take medication and go to therapy, anything to get out of that place.

I kept my word and began to put my life back together. But it was like fixing a broken clay pot in the dark. I did a reasonable enough job to be weaned off the medication and even got married. But marriage turned out to be too much for me to handle. The stress quickly sent back into another episode, and I resolved to take medication in secret, worrying that it would make me appear weak in front of my wife, having to rely on meds to keep control.

Looking back, it's obvious that the relationship was far from healthy and it eventually collapsed under its own weight. Yet again, I was left with a pile of broken pieces that used to be my life.

But this time was different. This time I knew my triggers and my pitfalls. I had traveled down this broken road alone and in the dark many times and wasn't about to falter again. I kept good people close to me, I went to therapy, got into shape and even began to volunteer my time. Anything to keep me from losing control again.

All my losses had lead to this moment where I could build a man that I could say was a worthwhile human being. All the voices that used to vie for control had choked off one by one, and amidst the storm, I was able to find a light and make my way safely to shore.

* * *

Realizing I'd gone silent, you look up from the cracked piece of tile you've been staring at, wondering if that's the end of the story, only to realize a small smile plays on my lips.

"That's not the end of the story," I say, and you wonder if I've somehow read your mind. "While volunteering, I met the most wonderful woman I've ever known—fell madly in love and got married. About a year later, we bought a house. Between buying the house, moving, car problems, and a family issue, the stress began to pile up. I could practically smell the illness trying to sneak its way back to the forefront, like a fairy fart under a cellar door.

"My wife, Laura, being the wonderful woman that she is, was patient and understanding. We took some time to ourselves, and she made sure I had what I needed to get my balance again."

I stop talking again and look around the room at all the empty chairs. You follow my eyes and realize where this is going.

"So, why," I begin again, "After all I've been through, are we here, alone? Because the life I've lead has taught me not to trust people. Time and time again I've been betrayed and hurt whenever I've opened up about even the tiniest of things. And this.... This is one of my biggest weakness of all. Or so I thought...."

I look down for a moment, ashamed. For the first time, you

stand up and make your way over to me, and the words rise in your throat, "What happened?"

I look back up, my eyes wet with tears. "My wife spoke five words to me... 'You're gonna be a daddy...' I knew that schizophrenia was genetic, and I was terrified of my child growing up the way I did, or being ashamed or embarrassed of me. I wasn't about to allow that to happen. It was time I embraced who I was and accept whatever came my way. No matter what happens, I'd been through worse. But more than that...."

Suddenly, the dimly lit room brightened and there, in the shadows, were dozens of others listening and smiling.

"I wasn't alone."

Those that had been hidden, make their way to the seats—some stop and shake your hand or pat you on the back.

"There's a whole culture of people just like us out there, waiting to be supportive and helpful, reminding us that we're not alone in our struggles. Ever. I drew something special to tell the world about my illness and while there were some who faltered, ignored or denied, the majority of my friends, family and even people I hardly knew came out with positivity and love. And that is the world I'm happy to live and raise my children in..."

MARS ANDRAS

"You're a joke. You know that, right? No one likes you, and if no one likes you, they for sure won't like your writing. Your story is shit. Your writing is shit. Give up now before you embarrass yourself."

That's my anxiety talking, or maybe my depression. It's difficult to tell sometimes. Either way, they're both total bitches. I can go from caring too much to not giving a shit in the split of a second. It's fucking exhausting.

It wasn't always like this. I used to get excited about things. Genuinely excited. Not the "excited" that I get now, where something good happens, and I wait for the inevitable — that something else will come to take it away. I used to be genuine, maybe I still am.

At the beginning of 2016, it became clear that it was time to start telling my story. I'd wasted the last twenty years feeling sorry for myself. I don't have any more time to fritter away living in the cozy shell I've build up around myself. It was time for me to not only be honest with myself, but with the rest of the world. Maybe my honesty would help others going through the same issues.

With that being said, it was never my plan to write about my childhood. At least, not yet. I thought I would ease myself into it by talking about my mental illness, starting my story right after my mother died when I was seventeen. After she had died, I was diagnosed with depression and anxiety, with a touch of borderline personality disorder mixed in. Because, why not? I already knew I had depression and anxiety. My college freshman psych class taught me that much. When they brought up borderline, I told my therapist to "fuck off," and never went back to therapy. I don't know why exactly. I suppose it's because, as far as mental illnesses goes, depression and anxiety seemed "normal," manageable. Borderline meant that I might actually be crazy, and I just couldn't deal with the thought. While I find this piece of my story the most interesting, it's not what the world is necessarily interested in, which I find unfortunate.

No one wants to know that I sometimes sit up at night because my mind won't shut off, or that there are days when I don't want to get out of bed because, why bother? That stuff's not sexy. It's real. Having panic attacks while grocery shopping isn't me just "overreacting." It's me being overwhelmed by the emotions of others swirling around me. This is why I used to drink A LOT. Drinking numbed the part of me that was so affected by others. But most people don't want to hear about that. At least, not yet.

Once I started writing, I learned quickly that when people find out your mother died of early-onset Alzheimer's disease, they don't want to know about what came after. They don't want to know that you once thought about killing yourself in a boyfriend's bathtub out of spite. They want to know what it was like to grow up with Alzheimer's in your life. And maybe I knew that in the back of my mind, but I was too scared to admit that I was ready to share that part of my story. It's much easier to write about what an asshole I was in my twenties than to actually write the words: my mother forgot me.

Being ready to share any part of my story terrifies me. It means I've evolved into someone who gives a shit.

MATTHEW WILLIAMS

I WAS 31 when I was first diagnosed with mental illness. I never ever expected it to happen to me (does anybody?), and it certainly wasn't a label that I wanted.

I had known that something was seriously wrong. Happiness, even for a moment, became harder and harder until it vanished altogether. I didn't know where it had gone, nor where, or if, I could ever find it again. And as more and more days became trials to be endured, night after night became a waking nightmare of imagined fears. That's when I realised it wasn't going away anytime soon, and I wasn't going to overcome it alone.

And yet...and yet....it was difficult to take the steps that I needed to take to get help. After being diagnosed with depression, I continued to work despite being advised by a number of people around me that I needed to take some time off. My confidence was shot to pieces and my ability to do my job was waning. Yet, I felt that I had to battle through it—that taking time off would be admitting defeat.

I was afraid of being labeled.
Matthew Williams, mentally ill.

I was, of course, aware of mental illness, but in my 30 years, I had never knowingly encountered it. I wasn't a judgmental person and didn't carry negative perceptions of people that suffered mental ill-health, but I was very aware of the social stigma that existed. And I was afraid. Not only of the label, but of what it would mean for my future, presuming that I was to have one. How would it affect my career? Who would employ me now that I was labeled as mentally ill? Who would trust me in a pressurized role?

It's natural to be concerned about what others think of us, but this shouldn't have to come at the cost of not doing what we need to do to take care of ourselves. It strikes me that I wouldn't have had these concerns had I been suffering with a physical health issue—all that would matter would be getting better, and I wouldn't doubt that my friends and family would do all that they could to help me to get back to full health.

I'm not looking to compare the nature and severity of physical and mental illness here, nor suggest that one is more serious than the other, but it cannot be doubted that relative social perceptions of physical and mental health differ greatly, as do the resources allocated to tackle each of them.

The associated stigma that exists around mental health was very much in my mind when struggling to persist at work in the direct opposition to my declining mental health. My confidence was shot to pieces and routine tasks became terror-filled ordeals, each charged with the potential to cruelly confirm me as a failure, as a fraud to be exposed. I continued to struggle, day after day after day, until I experienced a very painful, very public break-down at work. Not my finest hour.

The most difficult thing about my depression was how it changed me so completely, so totally, into someone, no, something, that was utterly alien to the me I'd always presumed to be. One memory from this time remains vivid in my memory: a member of the local crisis team visited me at home and as he talked he asked me to tell him who I was. I couldn't answer.

Who was I? Or rather, what was this thing, this shell that inhabited the space where Matthew used to be? Unable to answer, I turned to a photograph of Matthew holding his newborn son, smiling. 'That's him.'

This loss of self of the sufferer makes life very difficult for their loved ones too, as they too are unable to recognise this stranger in their midst. No matter how loving, supportive and understanding, little that they say or do seems to provide any comfort or consolation to the sufferer, entombed as he or she is within the confines of their own private hell. Little can penetrate the abyss, and the futility of effort can sap the spirit of the most devoted loved ones.

And as important as it is for the sufferer to never lose hope that this too shall pass, so too is it important that loved ones maintain faith that the storm will subside. For when that day comes and the former sufferer has regained their capacity to feel, to love, and to participate once more in the routines of daily life, a special place will be reserved in the heart for those that were there no matter what.

The toll that depression can take on relationships with loved ones should not be underestimated, and from understanding this, we can perhaps glimpse an insight into the perverted mindset that can convince the sufferer that their loved ones would be better off without them. Far from a selfish act, from the sufferer's twisted perspective suicide can appear to be a longed-for release and not only for themselves.

In fighting the stigma that surrounds depression a greater empathy for sufferers and a greater understanding of their particular torment can save and ultimately help to rebuild broken lives. When facing an opponent that is so determined to break the spirit of an individual's suffering is compounded by stigma, which is fueled by widely held misconceptions. When questioning the sufferer's character; assigning blame regarding how and why the affliction should strike is like condemning the sufferer for a perceived willingness to allow the illness to take hold, as well as creating a misconception of whether depression is a real illness at all.

Once depression tightens its grip, the illusion of control over one's mind is exposed for the fallacy that it is. Depression is an equal opportunities affliction and it would be as well for us all to recognise this if we are to arrest its increasing incidence. According to clinical-depression.co.uk, major depression is,

"...a huge problem and it is growing. Major depression is the number 1 psychological disorder in the western world. It is growing in all age groups, in virtually every community, and the growth is seen most in the young, especially teens. At the rate of increase, it will be the 2nd most disabling condition in the world by 2020, behind heart disease."

If we are to arrest the rise of depression it would do us well to recognise that just as none of us are immune to a heart-attack, nor are any of us beyond the reach of depression. Just as the heart is an organ, so too is the brain; just as the heart can succumb to disease if we do not keep it healthy, so too can depression strike should we be complacent of the need to cultivate a healthy mind.

For far from being in control of our minds, perhaps it is instructive for us to consider psychologist Jonathan Haidt's metaphor of the elephant and rider:

"Our emotional side is the elephant, and our rational side is the rider. Perched atop the elephant, the rider holds the reins and seems to be the leader. But the rider's control is precarious because the rider is so small relative to the elephant. Anytime the six-ton elephant and the rider disagree about which direction to go, the rider is going to lose. He's completely overmatched."

This is why I speak out. This is why I refuse to be silenced by stigma. I know what happens when the elephant takes charge; I've seen and felt the devastation that can be left in its wake. But I've managed to re-take the reins and brought the elephant back into harmony with its rider. And by sharing our stories, by fighting against stigma, we can help others to do the same.

MEGHAN SHULTZ

UNRELENTING. Unforgiving. Empty. Hollow. Excruciatingly painful. Physically painful. Confusing. Heavy. Suffocating. Desperate. Lost. Isolated; this is what Depression feels like. This is how it makes you feel. It's hard enough to deal with these symptoms and with Depression as an adult, but what about when you were a kid? I had problems all through my childhood. I was predestined for a life with mental illness, I guess you could say. We are very old friends. But there was a point when it got noticeably worse.

I'm not going to bore you with my earlier childhood, I'm just going to skip right on ahead to when I was about ten years old. One night that year, I was drying the dishes after dinner, and I remember standing there in a half-light, just me by myself. I always dried the plates and cups first and left the cutlery and utensils for last.

I picked up a knife—it was some kind of carving knife I think. I held it in my hand as if to dry it but instead I just stood there, looking at it. As I was looking at it, I thought to myself, 'I could cut myself with this...'I could kill myself with this.' I don't know how long I stood there for, but eventually, I left the knife and went to my room. I don't know what purpose it is serving me but, sixteen years later, I still remember that night as if it were yesterday.

Maybe the reason I remember that moment is because it was 'THE' moment. It was the first time that I knew something was wrong. But I didn't know what. I was terrified. I was terrified because, at ten years old, I couldn't understand why I was having those thoughts. I couldn't understand why I would want to do that to myself. I didn't know that it was a mental illness. I was confused. Obviously, I jumped to the conclusion that something was wrong, and that I was 'defective,' but for the most part I tried to ignore it. But hey, we all know it's not that easy, right?

It got worse. Just kept getting worse. And worse. And worse. I was too ashamed to tell my parents. I was afraid that I would get in trouble for having thoughts like that. I kept withdrawing more and more. I was incredibly anxious, especially around people, and the thoughts of self-harm and suicide were persistent. I became a perfectionist in certain things, and when I wasn't the best, I felt even more like a failure. Just adding fuel to the fire, I was in so much pain. Honestly, thinking about it is making me cry. I wasn't even in High School yet, so I thought there was something wrong with me. I thought it was all my fault, and that I wasn't good enough. I felt that I deserved to die. I was in so much pain, I thought that death must be better than this. I didn't know I had a mental illness. I didn't know it wasn't my fault. I didn't know I was going to be okay because I didn't see a light at the end of the tunnel

I started High School when I was thirteen. This is when stuff got real. This is when I started cutting my self. I started off with less than scratches. I was afraid someone would see, but it escalated quickly. I wore a sweater every day, and I wore watches and bracelets all up my arm. I was so ashamed. I was starting to hear voices too. They made me very agitated, so I would talk back to them sometimes.

I started abusing over the counter pain pills since I found that they calmed me a little before school. I wouldn't take them every day, just some days. I started seeing people too—hallucinations— not real people. It reached a tipping point when I was fifteen years old. One night, I couldn't take it anymore. I felt more than just pain. I felt nothing. I gathered up every pill in the house and took them.

I woke up the next morning. I was so angry. and also incredibly sick. So, I went back to sleep. I woke up again around nine or ten at night, and by that point, I was so done with feeling sick. I got up and found my mum in the living room. I said to her, 'I think I need to go and get my stomach pumped.' She asked me why and I told her what I had done. She was angry, but not the bad kind of angry, though. I think that she was angry because she was afraid and upset.

When we got to the hospital, they set me up with my drip and all that jazz, then started inspecting me. My mum was sitting right there next to me when they pulled up the sleeve of my left arm, displaying all of the self-harm I had caused. Mum looked upset, but how could she have known? For five years, I had been so ashamed of myself—so ashamed of every little thought in my head. I was a master actor. Aren't we all?

Being in so much pain and not knowing why sometimes seems worse than the pain. As an adult with a now seemingly accurate diagnosis, I find it much easier to manage my pain during depressive episodes. I'm not saying it's a party, but it does make it easier knowing what I'm up against sometimes.

Not knowing what was 'wrong' with me, not knowing that I

had an illness…that was hard. I was so young, and I didn't know. I didn't know how to get help, and even if I did, I didn't know what kind of help I needed.

I've had an illness my whole life, but there is nothing wrong with me, nor has there ever been. I'm not defective or broken, and I don't have a reason to be ashamed.

My whole family is amazing—especially my parents. It was hard for them at first because they didn't know how to deal with my illness, but they made and make an effort, and I couldn't love them more for that.

If you feel suicidal, please don't ever feel like you're alone, because you're not.

M.C. MALETTE

THE FACES of mental illness put forward by the world never match mine. They're nearly always white rather than brown, as I am; they're generally wild-eyed or in the context of violence, or out of control. That's not how the people in my life describe me, and even those closest to me often miss or mistake the signs. My bouts of depression and anxiety arrive as surliness—a brooding silence that creates distance, which is appropriate since distance is the primary effect of my illness.

In memory of myself from an early age, I was cut off from others. I see a boy in a hospital bed inside a plastic-walled oxygen tent during a bout with asthma. *Sound muffled.* Doctors, nurses, and my parents were visible as they came and went. But touchable only through the zippers and plastic of the tent as I laid propped up in bed. I could read their concerned and sympathetic smiles, but they couldn't feel my visceral fear as I struggled to breathe and survive in a body beyond my control.

Growing up, my clumsy efforts at closeness resulted in pain: reaching for a soldier father now here, then gone, now sober, then drunk, and when he was at home arguing with and sometimes striking my mother. I remember reaching for a mother trapped in her marriage, in her dark, foreign skin, estranged from and judged by her Latin American Catholicism. Reaching for siblings caught like me in the no man's land between the warring parties who'd created us, siblings who survived by punishing one another's vulnerabilities; and the brown boy me yearning for someone to "tell me I'm okay" was endlessly vulnerable.

Only after I escaped to college did the fog of inaction descend. I was huddled in my apartment, listening to music or reading aimlessly, skipping classes for days and weeks at a time. Outwardly, I seemed normal; I made friends, dated, partied, and performed well enough academically. I wrote and wrote and wrote, which is what I think saved my life.

One Sunday, the student newspaper called (I was a journalism major and on staff) asking me to turn in a story that I had thought wouldn't be due for several more days. I got in my car, intending to drive to campus, but instead I headed east. In a direction away from my apartment, I crossed the city and left the town. I reached a two-lane highway, saw a sign reading "Tonganoxie 18," and drove. I imagined reaching Tonganoxie and going further. I would drive east as far as I could—to New York. I would sell the car and live on the streets if I had to. All I wanted was space, distance from everyone and every place I knew. Eventually, uncertainty ended my bid for escape. I made a U-turn and drove back to town—to college—to the newspaper office. I dragged myself through the reporting and writing for the story—my life and the emptiness inside me heavy as a leaden cloak.

Intimacy eluded me as I entered into relationships that were initially perfect, and then suddenly, inexplicably, all emotion inside of me would freeze. Disappearing and empty, I could never tell the other person what had happened within me because I didn't understand it myself, and I couldn't talk about the past—the fog swirling in my head.

Over the years, I sometimes wished for an end to the confusion —an end to life. For long periods of time, I've felt healthy enough to function, to love, work, marry, and raise my children. However,

I've also done damage to my loved ones while in the grip of that fog. I've spent time on medications that saved me, and I've spent time in therapy that improved my understanding.

I choose not to think of my mental illness as a "battle." The chemical balances and imbalances that swirl in my brain and whatever their cause may be are part of who I am.

With the compassion I have toward others—especially those in pain or deprivation—I owe largely to my brain chemistry. My respect for sadness and grief come from it. My appreciation for the necessary duality of life, my resistance to simplistic ideas of "good" or "bad," are also due to my mental illness. Sadness and grief are the seats of my politics, my spirituality, and my definition of myself as a writer.

Still, I don't call my mental illness a "gift." I am no Zen master, only a person who's caused pain and love, happiness and grief, and who's received the same. If my illness has taught me anything, it's that life is uncertain and defies an easy definition. So do I; so does my mental health.

My depression and anxiety are the circumstances of my existence, like my height, my near-sightedness, and my brown skin. They offer disadvantages and perspectives that others lack, depending on the situation. So, I don't fight the fog, and I don't love the fog. It's there. Inside and outside of me, passing through—emanating from me.

When I remember to take care of myself, to be kind to myself, we get along.

My real enemies are society's and my own limited attitudes: stigmas, baseless assumptions, ignorance, fear, and oppression, which flows from ignorance. They're my greatest burdens as a mentally ill person because they allow me to deal with my illness successfully. They limit and/or misdirect society's support for people like me. They cut us off from one another and from wider participation in the life.

I think about the day I drove towards Tonganoxie, and about how the day might have gone if I had been able to say, "I'm having some real problems with depression. I need some help with this story." I wonder about the difference if I had been able to name and talk about it rather than feel weak, broken, and ashamed.

In a way, I'm still on the road to Tonganoxie—never quite arriving. But I've gotten more okay with that in my 50 plus years, gotten more okay with being in the fog. With being there, still.

MIKE FIERRO - PART I

THERE'S BEEN a lot of talk recently about the stigma of mental illness. There's only one way to erase a stigma, and that's by shining a light on individual stories. This is mine ... I have Bipolar Disorder. I first showed signs of the disease in my teens, but wasn't diagnosed until last year. Don't worry about me, I'm fine. I'm the same person my friends and family have always known. In fact, I'm better now that I'm able to treat those few parts of me that never felt right. The more people talked about the stigma, the more it bothered me. So, if it helps to put a face on mental illness, use mine. I'm OK with that. And I'm OK.

So, I say I have bipolar disorder, and that's no bigger of a deal to me than saying I get migraines. They can both be debilitating and can both be treated with medication, both preventive and abortive medication. Oh, and neither one can be seen ... only felt by the afflicted. So, what's the difference? To the sufferer, there is none. But to our society, there's a huge difference. And that is bullshit.

I am (un)fortunate enough to have both migraines and bipolar, so I am a great test case. But from a symptomatic standpoint, I'd be hard-pressed to tell you the difference. I have laid in bed, holding my head, and cried from the pain of a migraine. I have done the same from the pain of my thoughts. I have smiled and laughed and slapped people on the back when I feel better after a migraine. I have done the same when my mood shifts to mania. Back up a sec, you may not know what mania is. If there's going to be a story about my bipolar, it probably warrants a brief definition:

Bipolar disorder is characterized by extreme mood swings lasting at least a few weeks each (or as my last one did, 14 months). The swings are episodic in nature, meaning they're not always there. The two sides to the bipolar coin are mania (in its simplest form "up") and depression ("down"). As in any part of life, things are rarely this simple. The depression part is fairly straight-forward. It's more than "being a little down" – it's a soul-sucking certainty that nothing matters, it's impossible to do anything, and even the smallest tasks, like getting out of bed, seem damn near impossible. It's taking the side roads home because you're afraid the temptation to crash your car on the highway will be too late. Yeah, it's that. The manic side is harder to define. For some, it's periods of great creativity and production. For others, it's agitation and anger, and for some, it's a feeling of impulsivity and pressure. And racing thoughts, we can't forget those.

I have been diagnosed as Bipolar I with Mixed Episodes. Ah, the mixed episode – the bane of every bipolar's existence. As you might have guessed, a mixed episode is where characteristics of both mood extremes show up together. It's perhaps the most dangerous type of episode there is (not to others, but to yourself). Imagine depression, anger, and impulsivity having a picnic in your head – you do not want to go near that lunch bunch!

Anyway, the year since my diagnosis has been an interesting one, to say the least. When they tell you that you have a mental illness, there's a bit of denial that goes on – I won't lie about that. But then there's a bit of comfort as you realize all the times in your life where you knew you were different, but didn't know how, have now been explained. That's easily the best part of being "cate-gorized" as something – knowing that your life (in your head at least) where you were the starring character as the weird kid in a teen movie … was just in your head. It also explains why I was always the funny guy – I've been a lot of things in my life, but the funny guy is a constant. I didn't always know this at the time, but sometimes that was because I was manic, and it came naturally, and other times, I was hiding depression because I forced it. Then there's a sense of loss. I was undiagnosed for 30 years – what might I have done differently if I'd been aware and treated? What pain might I have avoided? What pain might I have saved others?

Finally, during that first year, there were meds. It takes 6-12 months to find the right combination of medication to handle all the aspects of this disease for each patient. Mine took about 10 months, and these aren't little medications – these are powerful beasts with a list of side effects longer than Santa's naughty & nice list. One of them gave me diabetes (yeah, no shit!). One of them gave me all the symptoms of Parkinson's, but without actually having the disease (didn't know that was possible). In the end, though, we got to the right combination, and all is well.

So, what do I want you to know out of this tale? More than anything, it's that I'm the same person I've always been. There's no difference in me since I've been diagnosed; it's just that there's a new word that applies to me now. The other thing I'd hope you can take away from this is that not all mentally ill people are insane. Most, in fact, are normal people leading normal lives. Like me. You already know many more of us than you think.

MIKE FIERRO - PART II

SOMETIMES DEPRESSION SNEAKS up on you. You're just going about your day without a care in the world, and you realize there's a little tug at your heart that's demanding attention. As you look at the situation, you realize you've been growing more and more depressed over the last few days, and now, there's no denying it ... you are depressed. That's OK, you've been there before. You know it will work its way out and eventually go bugger someone else. Those are the nice depressions. The ones where you need to put the pieces together, because no one piece is big enough to declare itself your owner.

That's not what happened to me this time. And it's silly because I've known this was coming for months (or rather I knew this was one of the possible outcomes for months). I knew it was coming and I knew it would hit me hard. I underestimated it. I have been hit with a depression so sudden and so black that I have to squint to see the light. Draw the drapes and cover the mirrors, for the darkness has returned. Let no light shine on his face, as the only thing worse than his feeling is his countenance. It is better to lay in the dark, knowing he is there, beside you, rather than to ever stare into his face.

Fortunately, I've been here before. I know how to draw warmth from his cold fingers. I know how to masquerade for those who don't need to see a broken face. I know that I am safe. Most of all, I know that I am safe. He has nothing to offer me that could cause me harm. I can live with him, squeezing my chest for as long as he needs to stick around. He can go fuck himself if he thinks he can outlast me. I may be a broken warrior, but I am a warrior, nonetheless.

I remember a happy place ... I think there was a castle, or maybe a boat. Maybe even an island. It's all so fuzzy now. The happy memories are like barbs that stick in my soul. The gut-wrenching reality of today bonds my loved ones more than memories. I cry a lot, both for my pain and for others' – some of theirs is much worse than mine, and I don't know how they can bare it. My hope for them is that their defense mechanisms of numbness have kicked in.

Numbness comes with great depression. It is required to maintain sanity. Numbness kills all emotion and feeling. It's an all or nothing sort of thing. Feeling anything means feeling everything, and everything is unbearable. Sure, there are good feelings that we miss this way, and there are some bad feelings that we could probably handle, but it's the feeling that takes your heart and rolls it in broken glass that must be held down. There's no avoiding visiting that feeling for brief moments – just enough to remember why you're in the dark with that guy around your chest, but you can't have that raw nerve exposed to the everyday world. One simply cannot function with an open hole in their heart.

I should say here that I am OK. I am safe. I am not in danger. I am simply depressed at an unfathomable level. I didn't really write this blog entry for anyone but myself. If you've come along for the journey, welcome. But I needed to get this out of me. For me. Bleed the poison a bit ...

NATASHA BOUNDS

"I can't do this anymore. I can't help you."
"You just want me to admit that I am broken! You are looking for a
reason to leave."
"No. I am looking for a reason to stay."

NOT EVERYONE CAN LOOK at the exact moment when their lives changed. I am lucky. My partner, Gray was brave enough (or tired enough) to say what needed to be said. He has stood by me every day since then and I will be forever grateful.

Of course, it didn't start there. I was a shy child. That is what I thought, my parents thought, even teachers. Twenty to thirty years ago I would have been called a good kid. We didn't diagnose children back then with social anxiety.

In my early twenties, I was diagnosed with a peptic ulcer. That was the start of a twenty-year battle with myself, my high-functioning depression, and anxiety.

At twenty-nine, I had my first panic attack. I had six more within the next six months. That is when I talked to a therapist. Therapy didn't last long. I figured I could control it with yoga and diet. I wasn't someone who needed medication or professional help. I wasn't THAT bad. That wasn't me. So, I learned to control my diet and to do something physical, and take prescription strength antacids to control the physical effects of my stress levels .

All the way into my thirties, I knew I had depression and anxiety. I just figured that since I got out of bed everyday and did the things I was "supposed" to that it meant I wasn't severe enough to really need help. I could handle it on my own. I just needed to suck it up and stop feeling bad. If other people managed it, I could too. That is what I thought. What I avoided facing were the people in my life that started to distance themselves.

I went along like this until I turned forty-three, having what I considered to be good days. While I can't say I was ever happy, things were status quo and that is what I thought life was like. I wasn't prepared for what happened next.

Gray and I were trying to figure out our relationship, and I was working on what I wanted to do for work throughout the rest of my life. We would argue (couples do that), but I noticed I would be unable to function the next day. He would tell me he loved me and my brain would tell me he was just saying that to calm me down. He would get upset because I had accused him of not loving me, wanting to leave, or whatever…because that is the story I was telling myself. He was going to leave—everyone did. It was just a matter of time, and I couldn't understand why he wouldn't either just tell me the truth or convince me I was wrong.

I didn't expect someone to challenge me. I didn't expect him to stick around and make me take a good hard look at myself. I didn't expect him to look for a reason to stay.

I made an appointment with my doctor the next day and decided to go in and be honest with her: I was having erratic and strong mood swings; I was sobbing uncontrollably for no apparent reason. I would suddenly get very angry and there were some days I couldn't do anything but sit on my couch and stare into space. I diagnosed myself: clearly I was emotional and lazy. She asked me some questions and diagnosed me instead with PMDD and depression.

I suddenly felt lighter. *You mean there is actually something happening with my brain chemistry?* Okay, well, I am still not "bad" enough to need medication. The doctor sat me down and talked to me about starting on a low dose of Prozac to help "take the edge off". I decided I would try. I had a follow-up visit four weeks later, and I had her take me up to the next dosage.

What I hadn't expected was that even a low dosage would take my anxiety down. It would almost stop the ruminations. I realized I had never really *lived* without those things. I had no idea I could. I found a therapist and he explained anxiety and dysthymia to me. He explained what happens when someone with dysthymia also has deep depressive episodes.

Now, two and a half years later, I have good days. I feel happiness. However, I still have bad days, too. I recognize them most of the time and can ask for help, and I get tired of fighting my brain some days, but I know that another good day will come.

Over the last year, I started to talk to people openly about my struggle. It helped me to let people know that some days are a fight, and to ask them if it would be okay to lean on them when I needed to. What I didn't expect, was the outpouring of people who were grateful that I had spoken up because it made them feel less alone. People began to tell me their own stories. Suddenly, instead of being alone, we had networks of people that we could ask for help, or even just for the simple comfort of a silly picture. People were surprised that I had been struggling.

Last year, Gray and I lost a dear friend to PTSD-related suicide. That was the last straw for me. The path was clear; I needed speak out whenever and wherever possible. Some days, writing posts, talking to people or just reminding someone they are not alone is what drives me. I want there to be better resources for people who are struggling, and I want everyone to stop fighting about whether medication is the answer or not. We need to be for better health coverage and making resources available to everyone so they can find what works for them. For example, medication doesn't "fix" me. It makes it possible for me to look at things objectively. Cognitive Behavioral Therapy and practicing mindfulness also play a huge role in managing my depression and anxiety. Those things won't work for everyone, but they have worked for me. Resources should be available and people should be able to find what works for them without the fear of ridicule. We live with enough fears.

Speaking without fear has played the biggest role in getting me here. It started with that conversation with Gray and continues every day with each person I meet.

NEESA SUNCHEURI - PART I

My MENTAL ILLNESS journey is a long and circuitous one. It began as soon as I could tell the difference between sad and happy. It now continues today, although I am fortunate and proud to be in recovery.

My father was an abusive person, both to my mother and myself. We always had to walk on eggshells around him because he was quick to anger. When the rage began, he would scream like a boiling tea kettle. Whenever this happened, I would run away, quick, into another room, and shut the door behind me. Curled into a little ball in a corner, I heard him screaming at my mother. It was muffled sound, words intelligible, and my mother never responded a single word. But the cruelty was absorbed through the door, easily enough.

From home, I learned that it was wrong to express my opinions and stand up for myself because it would make my father mad if he was in a bad mood. Often, he would ask me, "Your father is always right, is it?" And I would say, "Yes. You are always right."

When I started kindergarten, I took this lovely "skill" to school with me. Kids taunted me in the way kids do, which is normal enough. "Neesa the Pizza, you're stupid! You're too tall! Your hair is poofy and ugly!" But instead of ignoring them, or telling them to go away, I would just stand there, looking at my shoes. In my head, I thought they were right. Because at home, I learned that the best way to show a person respect was to acknowledge they were right all the time, even at the expense of my personhood. I strove to respect my classmates, and so I agreed with them that I was worthless.

As I got older, my lack of confidence worsened. I began to thoroughly believe that the word "LOSER" was stamped into my DNA and that it was a word written on my forehead, visible to all except me. I slouched terribly and was somewhat ashamed of being the tallest kid in my class every year. My mother didn't dress me fashionably also but instead opted for practical adult clothing from L.L. Bean. I was tall enough to wear it. Things got better in the sixth grade when my father left our home. I started therapy to help process my tangled feelings, but it wasn't enough. The damage was already done, and by the seventh grade, I wanted to die. To help me, my mother decided to pull me out of public school and put me into an alternative private school for eighth grade.

I'm very glad she did this. The school was very small, and there were only about twenty-five of us eighth graders. I started to enjoy school and come out of my shell. I continued therapy and had academic success. But then the depression started again, and by wintertime in ninth grade, I wanted to die again. This time, my mother took me to the hospital, where I stayed for two weeks. On my fourteenth birthday, I started new psychiatric medications: Zoloft and Klonopin. The stuff worked, and I stayed out of the hospital for the rest of high school.

I would be remiss in my story to downplay the importance of music in my life. I began playing the violin when I was five, and then switched to the viola when I was eleven. I played all throughout grade school and was among the class of accomplished pre-college musicians in my area, that big fish bowl called New York. I consistently was awarded principal violist in various festival orchestras, and sat principal chair at a prominent youth orchestra in Manhattan. After auditioning for conservatories for college, I was invited to attend some of the best programs in the country, one of which I ultimately attended.

As a musician, I learned to expect success for myself and strove to avoid failure as much as possible. This should have entailed practicing my butt off at all times, but sadly I was quite tortured in this regard. Due to my mental illness, I had problems with practicing for longer periods of time. After focusing for about a half hour, I would become overwhelmed with sadness, tears in my eyes. Always in my mind was the message, *You suck. You suck. You suck.*

It was hard to practice regularly when I thought I sucked all the time, so I avoided the instrument as much as I could. It was a miracle that I had the success that I did. But as I trudged through academia, I was very confused. Having studied music intensely my entire life, I defined myself as a "musician." And yet music was a source of pain. It made no sense.

For undergraduate studies, I desperately wanted to escape the East Coast, and go far away. So, I decided to attend a school in the Midwest. The school was perfect for me at the time. The campus was sprawling and green, and the downtown area was chock full of great restaurants. The music school was huge, and so it was easy for me to lose myself in the crowd and keep to myself. I was always surrounded by people in classes and orchestras, and yet I had few friends. I wanted it that way.

Why? I guess part of me wanted to immerse myself in my studies. I saw friendship and dating as a distraction, and I was emotionally fulfilled simply by music itself. The whole process of studying one-on-one with an esteemed professor was thrilling. I'd have an hour with the professor, during which I'd play a piece I'd prepared. Then he'd give me advice as to how to improve here, there, and so forth. Over the course of my degree, I studied with four different professors in this way.

There was just one problem. *I had to practice.*

When starting college, I was bright-eyed and optimistic. I

fancied that I would become one of the best violists in the school. But at the start of sophomore year, there was a viola competition that jarred me. Although my teacher advised that I not participate, another sophomore entered and won. I immediately then regarded her with hatred and envy, then resolved to "beat" her by winning next year's competition. This conflict was entirely in my mind. For the next year's competition, I entered and prepared diligently enough, but lost.

By this time, it was the end of my junior year in college. I realized that I was not becoming the best violist in the school and that I was unable to put in the hours of daily practice required to be of such caliber. Whenever I practiced, I would only be able to focus for about thirty minutes, when suddenly the thoughts came. *You suck. There's no point.* And then there were the thoughts without language. The emotions. The tears. I thought I was lazy and stupid, and I hated myself. I needed help, yet I didn't know how to ask for it or even describe it.

I started to think that there was some magical, spiritual quality that musical virtuosi had, that I didn't. And that if I were to cultivate this ability in myself, I would be the superstar that I always wanted to be. I incidentally befriended a student on campus who was a member of a meditation group. The group had a guru that lived in India, who was perceived to be a living Master akin to Jesus. I approached the group with sheer zeal and enthusiasm, feeling that this was my cure. I soon made arrangements to formally join the group.

In order to join, I had to have three individual meditations with a meditation leader, a person specifically appointed by the guru to lead meditation sessions both in groups and one-on-one. Before I started, there was one statement that should have sent off a red flag:

"The guru has said that people with mental illness should not do this practice."

I was earnest and upfront about my taking medications for depression. But my behavior was normal enough that I slipped under the radar. And anyway...how bad can a meditation practice be for a mental illness? Isn't it touted by even doctors, that mindfulness and relaxation techniques can help manage mental illnesses?

It was easy enough for me to assimilate the facets of this practice into my life. I meditated daily in the morning and evening, then held the guru in my heart as the cornerstone of my attaining Enlightenment. Every Sunday, during my senior year of college, I would hitch a ride to Indianapolis with a couple of disciples. We'd go to the home of a meditation leader and join their group meditation sessions. I also went on periodic retreats in different Midwestern cities, where I met many kind people. I felt my horizons broadening.

And I also believed that I was now on the way to becoming a virtuoso violist. Just ahead, I *knew* that I was going to get the praise and recognition that I so badly wanted and deserved. The chess pieces were being arranged. At the start of senior year, I joined the music school's baroque orchestra. I found new musical confidence, and I was introduced to a new set of musicians. Instantly, I developed a crush on one of them, a guy named Ricky*. I remained mum about it, although I was completely infatuated and "in love" by the end of the year.

During the spring of my senior year, I also worked with my psychiatrist to get off my medication, claiming that my meditation practice had healed me. I felt like I was on top of the world, like the productive superstar I always wanted to be. My schedule for the summer was jam-packed too. First, I performed at a music festival on my college campus, during which I squeezed in a fling with Ricky. Directly after this, I attended and performed at a six-week music festival in one of the southern states. After this, I took a trip to India on a spiritual retreat, where I meditated in the presence of the guru himself. Quite epic.

But all was not blissful. When splitting ways with Ricky, neither of us contacted the other, and the "passion" fizzled. Being off my medications, I started to decompensate while stuck at the music festival, and then I became obsessed with Ricky. In my heart, I *knew* he hated me, the same way I *knew* I was a loser in childhood. To numb myself, I abused Klonopin, even arriving at orchestral rehearsals in a sedated stupor. I eventually had my roommate hide the bottle from me, likely horrifying her. Then, when I traveled to India, Ricky was *still* on my mind, even when meditating before the guru. Where was my mental peace? Everyone had their eyes closed, and no one saw my tears.

The next fall, I returned to the same college to start my masters degree. I played in the same baroque orchestra, but this time it was torture. I thought of Ricky 24/7, and by mid-September, I started having violent thoughts about him. Completely spooked, I went to my therapist and told him Ricky's life was in danger. As I confessed, I cried my guts out. Suddenly, I felt like someone had punched me in the stomach. And as I dried my tears, I realized something changed.

Everything around me now had "energy." Whether it be a chair or a flower, everything around me began talking to me. Mind you, I didn't hear voices audibly, but everything around me now had personalities I could interact with.

I immediately perceived this to be a spiritual awakening. This energy I felt, I believed it to be what Buddhists call "chi." It was everywhere, and it was in my body too. It gave meaning to my life, where before there had been none. And it also gave me a new well-spring of inspiration in music. Practicing viola became a joy. *It's working...the meditation is making me a virtuoso.* I now viewed practicing as a sort of yoga, where the postures and technique of the viola were a path to Enlightenment.

But the chi was also confusing. All the people around me exuded energy as well, but it was more difficult to understand. People that I used to perceive as trustworthy and helpful would now exude energy that was hostile and vice versa. No one noticed anything was amiss though because no one knew me well to begin with.

At that time, I also auditioned for a music festival in New York

City and was accepted into the chamber music portion of the program. The festival was during the winter vacation between semesters. When the time came, I attended rehearsals and fulfilled my responsibilities, but my mental health was in shambles. Still, no one knew.

At home, I was obsessed with chi. I put mushrooms in my mouth, and it felt like they were exploding. I ran into the shower and rubbed oil on myself to enhance my chi. I wandered into stores, smelling the merchandise to see if products were heterosexual or homosexual, then I started to feel the "chi" in my body. I could direct it wherever I wanted. I felt powerful. I started eating lemons and going outside without a winter coat. I thought I could keep warm with the "sheer power of anger."

NEESA SUNCHEURI - PART 2

I WAS TAKING the subway when I finally broke down. I wandered into a pizza place, and then cried my guts out. Cops came and drove me to the hospital. When there, I got a new diagnosis of Schizoaffective disorder with bipolar features. They put me on meds and sent me home.

I finished the rest of the year in a daze. Halfway through my degree, I left college with no intention to ever finish. I returned home to New York, where I stayed with my mother. She had always provided sanctuary for me, and continued to do so then.

For several months, I didn't do much. I used the Internet to socialize with people, and I listened to Queen and only Queen. The lyrics spoke to me. In the winter that followed, I took a job as a violin teacher at a music store. I was a good enough teacher, so I decided to go back to school to become a K-12 public school music teacher.

About halfway through the degree, though, I began to break down again, but I was still taking my. This time, I thought I was the reincarnation of Beethoven. I went back to the hospital, and was forced to quit school. Yet again.

I then applied for disability and was accepted. I felt too exhausted to look for work, and I didn't even know what I wanted to do. I was tired of music, but music had been my entire life until now. I felt like I couldn't do anything else.

I began to simply float through life, which was okay at the time. Feeling creative yearnings, I wrote poetry and songs with guitar, which I performed at various open mics in the city. I became acquainted with many people, but felt excluded from social circles. I had become obese because I gained weight from a medication. I was probably excluded because of being unattractive, and due to my eccentric behavior. I was open about my illness.

Eventually, relapse happened again. I thought I was Beethoven, yet again. The in-and-out cycling through hospitals was becoming a way of life for me. A grim prospect, and yet a very real one. Hospitalization, release, inability to work. Still, I changed my diet, and was able to lose weight. I signed up for a kickboxing class to continue in this vein, but then became infatuated with the instructor within two weeks. The red flags didn't go off. After two months of this, I was convinced again that I was Beethoven, and that my instructor was my long-lost soulmate. I even proposed to him by giving him a little polymer clay pendant from Etsy.

Eventually, I took myself to the ER. While waiting in a room to be processed, I started to get commands from a voice claiming to be Barack Obama. He told me to retrieve my belongings from behind the security desk. Among my things, were journals I wrote, containing information that was the key to saving humanity. I followed his command, and then I blacked out...

I was then laying on the floor with about seven people trying to pin me to the ground. My arms and legs jerked uncontrollably as a blood-curling scream escaped from my throat. I was unable to control my body. It was doing these things without my permission. I started screaming that I was Beethoven. I was quickly injected with a sedative and then hoisted up onto a bed with restraints.

As they tied me down, I felt a sense of relief. I didn't want to attack anyone.

"I love you, I love you! Thank you so much." My mind was swimming with thoughts, and I was lost in psychotic fantasy. My arms and legs continued to jerk as I fell asleep.

I was then brought to a psychiatric unit. During this time, I was molested by a man about twenty-five years my senior. I didn't resist the flirting and attention from this guy, because he was overly assertive and bombarding. It was so wrong, though. The hospital did nothing to stop it either. I, suffering from schizophrenia, was forced to deal with a horny someone who had signed himself in due to stress. For him, psychiatric hospitalization was summer camp. So many people just don't understand.

After four weeks, I was discharged. But instead of enjoying wellness, I was immediately attacked by delusions and voices again. This time, a voice told me that I was the Anti-Christ, and I was personally responsible for the suffering of every creature that has ever lived. The voice tormented me non-stop, and at about 3:45 AM, I was commanded to leave my apartment. I had no choice but to follow. The voice told me to leave my keys on the floor outside my door so my mother could get in for my dog. Because I was about to die. That is what I was told.

I walked outside, and I felt my body wanting to throw itself into traffic. I was on the brink of losing control of my body again. I found a truck with a metal cart attached behind it, and I grabbed onto it for dear life. But then I started to fear that I would turn into metal. I could avoid death, but being a metal statue, living inside, would be a hellish punishment as well. No matter which way I turned, I knew I had a fiery, hellish fate awaiting me.

Suddenly, I thought I was a dog, so I peed in the street. I then realized I needed help. Luckily, I had my cell phone, so I dialed 9-1-1, and soon after, an ambulance arrived. I told them what happened and they drove me to the hospital—a different one from where I had just been, thankfully.

I stayed at this hospital for over two months. I was very ill, and progress was slow. The doctors put me on Clozapine. Although I improved, I kept having crippling panic attacks, which caused my treatment team to keep cancelling my discharge dates. After six weeks, I was given horrible news:

"We are applying for you to go to state. This is more permanent hospitalization. We think you can improve, but we have to do this because you have been hospitalized for a good amount of time already."

Frantic, I tried to figure out how I could get discharged. Remembering from before about a medication I took, which worked well, Effexor XR, I requested it from my treatment team. They did so right away, and the panic attacks began to go away. After about six weeks, I became well enough to leave. I felt like I had escaped a prison sentence. This experience was my first taste of mental health self-advocacy.

I must mention a certain person I met during my hospital stay: On two occasions, a woman named Trina* visited my unit and gave a presentation about her mental illness, sharing her story. She was a representative from NAMI, a not-for-profit organization dedicated to creating awareness for mental illness. Her story moved me. She also imparted a message that *recovery from mental illness is possible,* which I had never considered before. I was completely intrigued, and so I approached her afterwards. We exchanged information and kept in touch. I called her on the phone often, and she told me that I would see the light of recovery in my own life.

After leaving the hospital, I attended a partial hospitalization program, where I attended six hours of group therapy, five days a week. When this finished, I joined an IPRT day program where I remained for the next nine months. I befriended many friendly people and the program provided structure to my schedule. The groups ranged in topics from developing non-verbal communication skills to self-inventorying to see what jobs we wanted.

During IPRT, I heard about the career of peer specialist. A peer specialist is a mental health professional who has mental illness him/herself. The idea is that a person with mental illness can relate to people with mental illness better than a psychiatrist or social worker because they have actually gone through it themselves. I learned about a free-of-charge peer specialist training program at a place called *Howie the Harp Peer Advocacy Center*. I applied, and was accepted. I had no idea of what was in store for me. Miracles.

The program was intense. I had classes five days a week for five solid months. The commute was two hours each way, but it was completely worth it. I not only learned about the work of peer specialists, but I also learned the ways of mental illness *recovery*, and how to apply it in my own life. *Howie the Harp* truly changed my life, and gave me a passion and a voice, as well. I know now that I live for fighting stigma against mental illness.

After *Howie the Harp*, I did an internship at a great agency, closer to my home, thankfully. After the internship, I was hired to work there full-time. Now, I have been working full-time for a full year! It feels wonderful. In the past, I always felt beat up by my illness, and it went on relentlessly for so long that I felt I would never live a "normal" life—a life where I could work, earn money, and make meaningful, non-paranoid friendships with people. I have now accomplished my dream: being a productive member of society, but as I learn about "productivity," I have come to realize that a disability does not define a person. *Everyone* has value. *Everyone* deserves "kindness, dignity and respect." These three specific words were pasted to the top of the blackboard in the classroom at *Howie the Harp*, and these words ring true for all of us.

I think about my future now, and where I want it to go. I love my work as a peer specialist, and I have made my job into something unique and personal. I run an art group once a week, and I also write songs with clients. Now, my talents are being put to use! For me, performing on a stage where people pay to buy tickets... this doesn't change people's lives in a meaningful way to me, but bringing music to people who struggle with mental illnesses—people struggling against a society that denies our humanity...*that* is change. I want this to be the future—using art as a tool to enhance the quality of people's lives. Every person should have the right to creatively express him/herself. It is empowering and imparts a sense of self-worth and confidence. Everyone has a unique voice, and no one should be stifled.

I DID NOT CHOOSE TO HAVE BORDERLINE PERSONALITY DISORDER

RISA SUGARMAN

UP AND DOWN. Energized and then extremely sad. It's feeling happy, content, irritable, and agitated one moment later. Sometimes there is a trigger, sometimes it simply happens. It is very clear to me why Borderline Personality Disorder (BPD) is difficult to diagnose. The similarities to Bipolar Disorder can make it tricky. Recently, I even wondered if I really have Bipolar Disorder but I see now that it truly is Borderline Personality Disorder. I am frustrated though. The mood swings which can change five times within one hour are exhausting and sometimes debilitating. Yes, I can use the great skills I am learning in my DBT group but sometimes, I choose not to, which is called being "willful." Everyone is willful at times and I am when I am angry, upset, and feel as if I don't care anymore. This is when I may challenge my therapist with anger and irritation only to then feel tremendous guilt and sorrow hours later when I realize my behavior was inappropriate.

As Shari Y. Manning states so clearly in her book, Loving Someone with Borderline Personality Disorder, those who have BPD "are like sponges for pain." We take on the negativity which then brings us to utter hopelessness. My emotions scare me, and I often feel so out of control that my emotions are out of control.

Then, there is the fear, which can be constant at times. I'll fear for everything and everyone. It is all encompassing. My thoughts move swiftly and my mind does not rest. By late afternoon, I am already exhausted, and only recently, have I truly realized that living with BPD is exhausting in every definition of the word. Mentally and physically, it saps my will and my strength. While it was better controlled over the past couple of years, it does not feel so now. It coincides with going off one of my medications, which caused dizziness and nausea, so I will not be re-starting it.

It is very frustrating to be unable to use my skills. While there are times when I simply do not care enough, there are also times when I want to use them, but struggle to do so. Again, this is not how I want to be. The past several weeks have been a kind of an awakening for me, though. How I have been feeling these past weeks was once my everyday reality. Since a couple of years ago, this is how I lived, day in and day out. I just did not know that it was unhealthy and/or that it could be changed. Perhaps, this is why my frustration level is so high right now. I know I can feel better, I'm just not sure how to make that happen.

For those who either do not understand BPD or simply believe it is a made-up illness, I challenge you to try to understand the biology involved. I would never choose to live like this, having quickly changing moods and sporadic self-hate. Who would? This is why it is so important to educate people about BPD. It is a complicated illness and, yes, it is a real biological illness. I am not ashamed of it, and I will continue to work through it in therapy with medication. It is a heavy load to carry, and I cannot imagine anyone wanting to carry it along with the stigma. Having BPD is exhausting, and it preys on every characteristic of who a person is. It can be relentless, mean and lead a person to believe the evil thoughts it pulls in. This is not a "chosen" illness...I never asked for this. Who would?

EMDR, PPD & SELF COMPASSION...

STEPHANIE PAIGE

EVERY MONDAY, I have my therapy appointment. This is for my new therapy that I started a few months ago—EMDR (Eye Movement Desensitization and Reprocessing). If I tried to explain the exact technique, I think I would confuse you further. What I can say is: it is hard. It was extremely hard in the beginning, recounting memories that often brought me to tears and hyperventilation. Yet, I give this form of therapy two thumbs up as I have slowly and gradually begun to forgive myself.

My therapist has been all over my head in the last few months, starting with my recent severe depressive episode to my blocking belief that I don't deserve to get better. While the latter is no more an issue, I have yet to return to everything that has happened a little over a year ago.

As we have progressed in therapy, he and I have realized that my Postpartum Depression and Anxiety affected this latest and greatest episode of Depression. So, we dove into that time in my life.

My therapist asked me to sum up my whole Postpartum Depression and Anxiety episode and then determine which memory is the most painful. It wasn't too easy to choose.

Those months were a time frame I would like to forget, and one I thought I was emotionally over. I was not. Thinking back, the most painful memory was myself, sitting in the ER with my mother next to me, waiting to be seen.

It was the old ER, as my local hospital has recently been renovated—low ceiling and beige walls. The office chairs had grey fabric and black, plastic handrails. The room felt so small and was pure chaos. To the right of me, there were check-in stations with the workers behind a half wall of glass above the desks. To the left of me, there were more of these common office chairs filled with other people waiting to be seen. In front of me, there was a wall with a floral framed picture, and then the entrance to the ER was to the front left.

Although the other people in the room were talking and moving, I was slightly out of my body in my own pure hell that I was still unaware of. My main reason for going to the ER was for the simple fact that I must be malnourished and dehydrated since everything that went in my body quickly came out. I was rocking back and forth, with my hands gripped so hard on the handrails that they were in pain. In addition to this, I was shivering as if the temperature had dropped to zero degrees Fahrenheit. Hyperventilation was present and tears streamed out of my eyes, non-stop.

"When did this happen?" my therapist asked.

"Exactly one month after Sophia was born," I said.

"Let's go with that," he said. That was my cue to close my eyes and allow the Thera-Tappers to do their work. Buzz in my left hand then my right, repeatedly. I started looking at Postpartum Stephanie, and as anxiety churned my stomach, I could feel tears well up. I wanted to hug her.

"What do you feel?" he asked.

"Sadness for her. She must have been scared. She has never been through this before."

"Been through…," my therapist encouraged.

"The intense anxiety, the panic attack. This is new. All my bouts before were just Depressive. This was my first experience where anxiety made an appearance."

"What do you think you needed back then? Someone to have done something for you? Said something to you?"

The first round of EMDR with this question stumped me. I had the support of my family. I was seeing a psychiatrist and a therapist. I was on medication. What did I need back then? What would've helped me? We tried again, and instantly it came to me:

"I needed someone who had been through Postpartum Depression and Anxiety to tell me everything would be okay. I would've believed that person because they would have experienced what I had, or something similar. All these other people telling me it would be okay didn't help. They didn't know what I was going through. The Postpartum Community was so small back then (almost nine-and-a-half years ago)."

My therapist continued, "Put yourself in the ER, yourself now. Think about it. What are you doing? What might you say to yourself now."

He turned the Thera-tappers back on. I closed my eyes and returned to that scene. The present me was kneeling on the floor of the ER with my hands on the knees of the postpartum version of me. I could still see myself rocking back and forth. Truly scared for myself because I had no idea what I was going through. My current touch, an instant connection to the feelings inside of my head then. I tightened my squeeze and looked up at my old face. I focused on the blank stare I had on the wall ahead as I rocked back and forth. I noticed the fear in my mother's eyes at that time, as she wondered what was going on with her child. I turned back to the postpartum version of my face and spoke:

"It will be alright. You will be okay. I know you will be okay because I've been there."

The second I said, "I've been there," the postpartum version of me focused directly on the current me, and the old version of me stopped shaking. I kept repeating my words over and over: "I know because I've been there."

It was the first time I showed my postpartum self some self-compassion.

STEVEN ALEXANDER

HAVE you ever had someone say something hurtful to you, and it sticks with you all day long? It's hard enough dealing with one person saying hurtful things to you, but to deal with yourself is a totally different matter.

That's what my depression is; it's the voices of my two worst enemies berating me day in and day out. One of those voices is my most recent ex, who will remain unnamed. Why? Haven't you ever seen Fatal Attraction? I'm not putting myself through that! My ex —we'll refer to her as Miss S—often brings up how thoughtless I am, how I gave up a great person for her, how I am fat and ugly and dumb. She is like a parasite. She buried herself in my mind, and she still hasn't crawled out of my ear or nose in three years. Three years, I have been like this. Of course, I have always suffered from depression because of that other voice in my head. That other voice is me. I have always had self-esteem issues, and most likely always will.

Have any of you ever heard the song Make Me Wanna Die by The Pretty Reckless? The first half of the chorus goes:

Your eyes, your eyes, I can see in your eyes, your eyes/Everything in your eyes, your eyes/You make me wanna die/I'll never be good enough/You make me wanna die/

That's exactly how I feel. I feel that I'll never be good enough. I wasn't good enough for Miss S, I wasn't good enough for anyone before her, so how can I be good enough for anyone else? If the Devil doesn't think you're worth it, why would the angels?

I feel tortured like I'm drowning. I keep kicking and moving my arms, but my fingertips barely graze the surface. I'm always in reach of air, and just when I am about to reach it, she pulls me under again. So, I resort to hurting myself.

Why would someone that's hurting, hurt himself? I wish I knew. I am so tired. I am weak. I am ready to give up. I've attempted suicide multiple times throughout my life, and now have a few permanent scars because of it.

Verbal abuse is a real thing. I have been made fun of because I have mentioned being abused before, and it's verbal, not physical. Physical abuse does a lot of damage, but verbal abuse stays with you and destroys you slowly from the inside out. Many times, I feel like if I screamed at the top of my lungs, no one would stop to help; no one would care. They would just keep on with their business, and I would slowly slip into insanity.

There's one other thing that happens to me in times when my depression gets really bad: I see her. I see and hear my ex as if we never split up, and everything she says is degrading and hurtful. Her only purpose in life is to hurt me. I even have shouting matches with her often. That must really turn heads. You know what's craziest, though? There was a time when I thought I couldn't live without her. Now I'm forever stuck with her inside my head

Some days are better than others, some days are worse. Sometimes, all I do is pace the room and consider every type of death imaginable. I could hang myself, shoot myself, cut myself, throw myself down the stairs, lay down on a moving saw, stab myself, eat rat poison, drink bleach, fall asleep with a bag over my head, suffocate myself...the list goes on. I literally pace back and forth, considering every form of self-harm, death, and torture imaginable, and then I try to find a reason to not go through with it.

Sometimes my mind turns against me, and I convince myself that the positives in my life will turn to negatives and that there's no reason to believe in hope—no reason to go on.

My friends have always left, and surely they'll continue to...right?

Everything dies, which means my dog won't be around forever, and when that happens, my depression will worsen...right?

I failed Statistics twice, so there's no point in going back to college...right?

It's constantly one thing after another, and then I finally find that one unchanging constant and cling to it. Will the constant ever change? Maybe. But right now, I can always count on her. She calms me, makes me feel wanted, makes me feel loved. She's my best friend in the world. Sometimes, I worry about remaining attached to her because I am afraid, she too, will be gone one day, and I'll be left alone once again.

One thing I have realized, though, is that you can't live in fear. Fear and worry will make you old and ugly. Trust me, I feel and see that every day when I look in the mirror. Speaking of which, I only have one mirror in my house, and that's in the bathroom. I think that's because the one person I hate more than my ex, is me. The real battle is against myself. I sometimes feel like I'm split in half and my two sides are always at war with one another.

Some day, the pain will stop. Jesus put me here for a reason, but I don't know what that reason is, and sometimes I don't care. There are times when I want death more than anything, and there are times when I ask Him for help, and soon thereafter, I'm okay.

I've been told that I carry the weight of the world on my shoulders, and that I try to help everyone, then I become destroyed when I find that I can't help that person.

What can I do? What can I say? How can I get better? Am I fooling myself? Will I always be this way? Will I never be happy? Will I never be at peace while in this body? Will I ever gain control?

Or, am I fated to an insane asylum, arguing with my ex for the rest of my life?

THE NUMBNESS IN MY BLOOD

VALARIE KINNEY

IT STARTED FOURTEEN YEARS AGO, and now I am a different person.

For a long while, nobody could figure it out. My toddler son would have spells where he struggled to breathe, and sometimes turned a ghostly shade as he fought for air.

They diagnosed him with croup at first.

However, the croup never went away fully, and then it would come back with a vengeance. When my second son was born, and had breathing issues, things started getting really strange, really fast.

They were both sick often, and it took some time–several doctors, and a multitude of tests–to narrow down the problem. Once we had a few firm diagnoses, there was collaboration between the doctors, and then a flurry of treatments began.

At first, I was the same person I'd always been.

It hurt me to force my babies to take medications and hold them down for breathing treatments. I worried incessantly that my actions would traumatize them, though I didn't have a choice in the matter. They needed their medication or they couldn't breathe.

It clawed at my insides each time they went back for surgery, and acid would lap at the back of my throat until a physician came out to tell me everything was okay.

Overnight stays in the hospital with the kids made me feel panicked as though I was in some foreign land where I barely understood the language, but it didn't matter because nobody talked to me much anyway. I couldn't sleep, and eating at the hospital was limited to mainly graham crackers from the parent snack room.

I was anxious, and as a result, I often broke out in hives for no reason. I also threw up quite often, though not on purpose. I struggled to sleep for more than just a broken hour here or there, lest one of my boys stop breathing in the night.

I cried.

Another of my children was diagnosed with the same disorder the boys had, and everything felt so much more difficult.

It seemed, for so long that I was on this train in a tunnel that would never end, until finally it did, and now I am different.

The kids still live with chronic illness, and we still make a trip each month to the pediatric infusion pod at the hospital to spend several hours getting their infusions.

They still need medication daily, though over the years, their meds have changed.

This scenario is likely going to last forever.

I used to fight against that thought, but I don't fight it anymore. I accepted it a long time ago.

I think that's when my heart began to harden, and my thought process changed.

I no longer lurch at the sight of my children's blood, spurting from a bad IV placement.

My chest doesn't clench when one of them gets sick.

My eyes don't water when I give my youngest son his injection each night, though, the first time I had to do it, my hands shook and I felt ill at the thought of pushing a needle into my own child's flesh.

I don't cry much anymore.

I've talked with other mothers of chronically or seriously ill children, and this seems to be a weird theme with us all.

Perhaps, it's some sort of built-in coping mechanism, much like the numbness that follows the death of a loved one. The numbness has gotten me through many years of handling hard and horrible medical situations with my kids, but I sometimes worry it has changed me so much that I no longer feel things normally.

It's a thing I think about at night when thoughts get to be too much.

Is it normal for a mother to inflict a needle on her child without flinching, and instead do it as easily as she does the dinner dishes?

Toda, we drove the seventy miles south to our university hospital where my children receive all of their specialty care. Our regular nurse wasn't there, and a new nurse was in her place. She was having a difficult time getting my youngest son's IV placed, and when she finally got the line working, it was flowing rather slowly. She had him hang his hand with the IV in it off the edge of the table to fill the vials for his labs. As gravity did its job, the blood began to rush out.

Deep red splotches hit the floor, and I watched as my son's face turned a pasty white color. The situation got away from the nurse quickly, and crimson fluid was flowing everywhere, it seemed. Her gloves were smeared with it, and at one point, she held the tube full of my kid's blood out toward me and asked me to cap it for her.

I did it without thinking.

A tiny, logical voice in my head told me I should be upset at the sight of my son's blood on the floor (or the blood all over the nurse's hands, or at the fact that I was calmly capping off a vial of his blood like I'm his damn doctor instead of his mom), but that's all it was; a quiet voice. I felt no anxiety about it, no sadness that my thirteen-year-old son had to sit through this procedure again, like he and his siblings have done every month for the last ten years. I asked if it hurt, and my son–stoic as always–said no, and that was the end of it.

It's simply the way our life is now, and the fact that this doesn't bother me...well, bothers me.

I wonder if there is a name for the way I feel—if it's possible that so many years of living in medical crisis mode has traumatized me in a way I do not understand, and if I might ever go back to the way I was before.

I wonder if the numbness will ever go away.

THE WIND

VALARIE SAVAGE KINNEY

IT DIDN'T HAPPEN RIGHT AWAY.

After my second daughter was born, I was elated; absolutely over the moon.

My baby was beautiful.

My baby was perfect.

My baby screamed.

She screamed through the night, and kept my one-year-old daughter–and me–awake.

She screamed after eating, and I tried changing my diet to see if something in my breastmilk was upsetting her.

She screamed when I dressed her, when I rocked her, when the swing stopped for three seconds.

My husband worked third shift, so I didn't sleep much—short thirty minute intervals—an hour or two if I was particularly lucky. Many nights I slept only as long as the baby swing kept rocking, and would lurch awake to rewind the crank every fifteen minutes.

It was after a couple of months of chronic sleep deprivation that it began to happen: the Wind.

It was the sensation of being unable to catch my breath, the feeling that a great wind was blowing so hard in my face I could not breathe. I realized something was wrong because I was inside the house with the windows shut. It was snowing outside and there was no hint of a breeze in the house, not even a fan.

My baby screamed and I felt paralyzed because I could not find any air.

I did not tell anyone about the Wind. I did not know how to explain myself without sounding like I'd lost my mind.

The sleepless nights continued, stacking up on top of one another like the building blocks my toddler played with as her sister cried.

I read articles in magazines about parenting, about how to lose the baby weight and give enough attention to my toddler while caring for an infant. I read about getting a nutritious dinner on the table every night at the same time because routine is so important for young children. I combed through these magazines religiously but never found a story about another mom who felt wind in her face when there was none.

My emotions were erratic, and I began to weep over things like the mountains of laundry that just kept getting taller, the desperate loneliness that made my bones ache, and the thought of how much energy I would need just to cook dinner for my family.

I wore fatigue like a heavy winter coat and it weighed me down until my limbs began to feel as if they were made of lead.

And always, always, the Wind was there, stealing my breath and roaring past my ears.

There was a small voice in my mind that whispered to me about asking my doctor for help.

There was a different voice that said if I admitted to feeling depressed, people would come and take my babies away from me.

So, I stayed silent, and the Wind grew stronger.

Everyone assured me that as my baby grew, she would cry less. She would outgrow the colic or whatever it was that made her scream so much. That did not prove true.

Every day, every night, her frantic screams continued. Every day, every night, I wept and tried to breathe.

Irritation over everything—the sun shining or not shining, the television being on or not being on, people talking to me or not talking to me—allowed a permanent feeling of anger to sit hot and angry in my gut, and I wished for the energy to act on the anger. I wanted to destroy something, just to get the feeling out of me.

But I was too tired to do it. I was too tired to do anything.

There was a day when my baby was wailing, and my husband was asking about what I was going to make for dinner, and I was standing in the kitchen with the Wind pummeling me in the face. My lungs ached for a deep, solid breath, but I was unable to get one, and my toddler daughter tipped over a cup of water on the floor.

I began to scream. I screamed and screamed and screamed, and found I couldn't stop. I felt so frustrated, angry, and depressed that even my skin hurt. I picked up a coffee cup and threw it at the kitchen cabinets. It shattered and tiny shards of the cup fell all over the floor.

Time seemed to freeze for a moment, then it started up again in slow motion.

Quickly, I stepped over the mess to move my toddler away from the sharp pieces of ceramic, and she jolted away from me with a look of utter terror on her face.

My child was afraid of me.

Of me. Her mother.

It took me several days after that to convince myself I needed to call my doctor, and when I finally found the courage to do so, I told the receptionist I needed an appointment because I was having headaches.

I could not bring myself to say I was depressed. I felt as if admitting it would mean I was an unfit parent, and I loved my daughters more than my own life.

I went to my appointment and spent a few minutes trying to describe to my physician the headaches I wasn't really having. Finally, I stared down at my hands and told her, "You know what?

I'm not here because of headaches. I lied. The truth is, I think I might have Post Partum depression."

I started taking Paxil and it took some time to tweak the dose and figure out the best time of day for me to take it. I had hoped the effect would be immediate, but it wasn't. Several weeks passed before I was able to emerge from the darkness, but bit by bit, the heaviness fell away.

One day it struck me: the Wind had finally stopped.

I took a deep breath, and smiled at my babies.

TO BE BOTH CLIENT AND CLINICIAN

VINCENT J. FITZGERALD

I SIT IN SERENE, soft light, and contemplate what is safe to share, and what I should withhold. My war against anxiety is fought on many fronts, and I am battle weary from its barrage of multiple manifestations. Across from me, a person waits for my offering on the subject, and before I speak, I extend an affirming nod to convey understanding of racing thoughts, crippling fears, and sensations of dying. I choose only to nod because in this therapy session, I am the therapist, and therapists do not divulge vulnerabilities to our clients. Sometimes we divulge our vulnerabilities to no one at all.

The walls in the safe house I have built for clients must remain sturdy as there would be no sense of safety should I reveal my frailties and self-perceived incompetency. My understanding stems from more than clinical experience. I have spent hundreds of hours in the other chair as my embattled relationship with anxiety predates acquisition of the social work license I was driven to acquire by witnessing my mother's depression and my father's anxiety. Each time a new client asks if I have experience with anxiety disorders, I nod and think, more than I would wish on anyone."

I was asked to write a bit about the genesis of my anxiety, and have narrowed its origins to my birth. I was born into anxiety, and it is my birthright. What has changed as I have aged are degrees of severity and levels of disorder. In 5th grade, it presented itself only as embarrassment. I was too mortified to inform teachers that I never learned to tie laces, forcing me to tuck them into the sides of my shoes rather than face a humiliating confession. I also refrained from telling my parents for fear that even they would ridicule me. There is no safety in the house of anxiety.

Afraid to fail, I never tried sports in high school, and avoided rejection by ignoring girls, deferring to the confident guys who had the smooth lines of bullshit. I was so frightened of being asked to dance at senior prom that I skipped it and tried to sound cool by telling people, "I don't do proms," rather than reveal awkwardness that also forced me to skip yearbook pictures. I have no memories of prom and am not immortalized on glossy yearbook paper. In college, I feared group projects and oral presentations. Weeks in advance, I predicted stuttering and spitting words, which would likely resemble languages created for Star Wars characters. These thoughts were anxiety appetizers before I was fed a foul main course of adulthood.

Parenthood was my first severe trigger of a disordered thought. When my daughter started walking, I followed her around in lockstep to ensure she would not bump her head or swallow small objects laying somewhere outside reality. When she graduated to solid food, I monitored her chewing and implored her to take small bites because I believed she would choke. Anxiety doubled when my son was born, and I depleted joy at amusement parks because intrusive visions of them being flung from rides haunted me. I was so crippled by imagining sickness that I skipped family outings to spare myself perseverations about their safety. My anxiety was misconstrued as apathy, and laid the groundwork for eventual divorce. All wars have collateral damage.

Social anxiety at my first job in mental health rendered phone calls in front of coworkers impossible. Convinced I sounded inept, I snuck them when my teammates were away. If one reappeared, I hung up and announced wrong number. Anxiety tried to convince me I had no business working in mental health if I was not mentally healthy, but my fear of stigma prevented me from seeking treatment.

After my divorce, parenting my children alone was too much to bear. Anxiety returned in the form of globus hystericus; the sensation of an invisible lump in my throat, resulting in relentless gag impulses and leaving me bedridden until my doctor diagnosed me with generalized anxiety disorder. He relieved my physical symptoms with Xanax. What I once explained as nerves and shyness, mutated into monstrous manifestations with each new stressor in my life.

Within months of getting my generalized anxiety somewhat under control, my bubbling anxiety erupted into a colossal panic attack as I suffered while my daughter rode shotgun, unaware of my internal explosion. When we arrived at her soccer tournament, I begged her mom to pick her up so I could cower home where I retreated to bed and impugned myself as a failed parent. I recovered by the next day, but was less fortunate when a second attack struck on my way to watch football with friends. The attack en route to a fun activity scarred my brain and kept me housebound for a week.

Attacks snowballed into a disorder, and it was weeks before I dared venture anywhere besides the nearby school, in which, I served as a school social worker. Driving to my kids' home was impossible; I stopped taking them on weekends without explanation, and I isolated myself from family and friends. After my Zoloft kicked in, I ventured to the home of a friend I had not seen in weeks. I was stung by stigma when he compared me to Howard Hughes and asked if I was "done doing the hermit thing." My disorder was mistaken for choice at a time when I was without choice. I cowered at the notion that I was mentally ill, and told him I was just "doing me."

I continue to weave through my anxiety obstacle course, achieving licensure to be the therapist I desired to be, while following my own therapist's request to pursue writing. To be a therapist not in treatment would feel hypocritical to me, and to normalize my clients' need for therapy, I share my experiences after a few sessions. I want them to know I am not only leading them into battle against their own mental illness, but I fight alongside them in unified brotherhood as well.

IS ADMITTING BEING A VICTIM OF CHILD SEXUAL ABUSE COURAGEOUS?

MATTHEW EATON

THERE ARE times I doubt this power as I look at myself in the mirror. I am still remarkably human. The hair fades in color and quantity. The waist still expands as if my stomach had a mind of its own. I still have flaws like discovering the bottom of a bottle a bit too often.

What makes me different than all the other fleshy funbags out there? Why is it a huge deal for me to admit I was molested twice by the same man? Who cares about my past when there is so much suffering in the world?

These questions have an obvious answer, and it isn't because I am a bitter old man with thinning hair. No, the stigma of surviving childhood sexual abuse is real and potent. We teeter on the edge of darkness, daring ourselves to jump into the abyss. We never see ourselves as humans, but as broken toys for demented demon.

Any voice is as strong as the wind, obliterating the single cloud on a glorious day.

I was abused twice. Once when I was seven, after my parents divorced. I trusted my family, and I was burned. My grandfather molested children for forty plus years, and I was one of his victims. My mother was another one.

The second time happened when I was thirteen. I was traded to my grandfather for about a thousand dollars. It almost destroyed me. However, other factors came into play to accelerate my youthful demise. I lied to my father about my abuse when I was fifteen. It would be the last time I talked to him. I lost the only home I knew on a lie. Everything I learned when I was a child was a lie.

I isolated myself from the world. The treasured burden was mine alone. I wasn't human. I was a monster. I was a glitch, ready for the scrap heap. I was unlovable, and I had the emotional scars to prove it.

When I was nineteen, I accepted my fate. I stared at the dark abyss and blinked for a moment. Suicide was the best option for a monster like me. It was time to erase the mistake and patch the glitch so the world could be better. I decided the ultimate solution was the best.

I made it out of that dark night with a vision, a promise, and a new way to look at life. It took me twenty more years to claw out of my isolated mindset. I faced the very question I asked at the beginning of this piece.

I sat on a bench three years ago, fired from another job and well aware I needed to change if I ever wanted to find peace. I explored the roots and saw I wasn't a glitch, but a mirror for the stigma my family carried with it for generations. We cherished it. We allowed it to ostracize us from those who loved us.

We didn't even love each other. We loved things more. We were obsessed with objects and money. We based our meager existence on the wages earned through tears and sorrow. I pressed into the fearful forest. I found I could hack away at the diseased branches and expose subtle truths about my upbringing.

I am only speaking up about my trauma now, but it is never too late to add a voice. My voice is needed, as is yours. We must stand for what is right and speak out against the stigma we have. No one should feel ashamed of their past. They should never be imprisoned by their fears and silenced by their shame.

You may not even believe you have the power to do something about the stigma. You might go through the same ritual in the mirror as I do. You might hope the steam from your morning shower hides enough of your face that you don't have to stare at it anymore.

You are lost in the isolation. You believe you aren't worth the effort. You still fall into the trap of losing something important. You fool yourself into thinking you can overcome this on your own.

I am not asking you to go out and seek help if you do not want it. I am not pointing you to a therapist as a magical cure for everything you've experienced. You have every right to stand in solitude. You have every right to carry on with what you are doing.

I chose the hard way to walk through life. I carried a stolen burden for two decades. My spiritual back was almost broken by the time I realized I couldn't carry it any longer. I had to give back what wasn't mine and move on with a lighter load. I speak about my two molestations and being traded for money because it helps me get rid of guilt that wasn't mine.

No matter what happened to you, you don't need to protect it anymore. The only thing you will lose is releasing the horrible truth you continue to hide. You might embarrass yourself with admitting it to start with.

The bravery you show by speaking can save a life. There is someone just like you staring in the mirror. They are asking themselves the same question I did when I came to grips with my stigma.

"Is admitting being a victim of child sexual abuse courageous?"

Yes, my friend; yes, it is.

THE LASTING IMPACT OF GROWING UP WITH ADHD

ROBERT VORE

THESE DAYS, it seems like ADHD is a punchline more than something people really believe in. But as much as I love a good 'SQUIRREL!' joke (hint: I don't), I have to admit that I'm just coming to terms with how much growing up with ADHD impacted me throughout my life.

See, I'm smart enough, and I don't mean that in a bragging way, just that I'm a great test-taker, and I'm usually pretty good at figuring things out. What I've never been good at, however, is focusing. Once I get going on something, I'm usually okay, but the initial focus-and-get-this-thing-started is something I simply cannot seem to get the hang of. Nowadays, that manifests itself in things like the rarity with which I post on this website. I tend to think of an idea to write about, and then can never seem to actually sit down and hammer it out. But growing up, it resulted in a near-consistent stream of zeros on homework assignments, projects, and major papers.

But the worst part of this wasn't the obvious effect it had on my grades over the years (they weren't good.) The worst part was feeling so frustrated that I was failing at things for no good reason. I knew it wasn't that I didn't know how or didn't understand the work to be done, I just could not for the life of me, figure out how to remember all my work, and actually focus long enough to do it.

I don't have a lot of very specific memories from my childhood, but I do have this one: Right now, I could drive you to the exact parking space outside of a Starbucks where I had a breakdown, crying to my mom because I was so frustrated. "I don't know what's wrong with me," I told her. "I don't know what's wrong with me."

Years later, after scraping my way out of high school and part of the way through college, I would see a psychiatrist. We would talk for over an hour about my frustrations and how bad I was at remembering things like how I literally couldn't do work if there was music with words playing. We also talked about how I felt like a failure because I'd always assumed I was lazy, too much of a procrastinator, and just 'not good at school.' He would prescribe me some medicine, and I would (for the first time), admit to the thought that maybe I needed some help in this area.

This is a fantastic story of present-day me: I take medicine, and I can focus on things I think are important. I'm in a Masters program, and I'm good at school, but that's not the main point of this post. The point I sat down to write about is this:

I still carry a lot of that with me. I still remember how frustrated I felt, how much I hated the moments when I would realize I hadn't remembered to do something or hadn't been able to focus on it the night before. I remember the dread that set in, every single time, when I took another zero.

I remember feeling like a failure. I remember thinking I was a waste, I was too lazy to accomplish anything. I remember countless talks with well-meaning teachers about how I was 'wasting my potential', that I just wasn't trying hard enough or 'applying myself.'

I remember hating myself for that. Having no idea how to change it, how to fix myself, how to be this better version of myself that I (and everyone else) wanted me to be.

And I'm willing to admit that I don't think a lot of that has healed yet. I'm twenty-six now, and if you asked me to make a list of the things I hate most, 'feeling like a failure' would make the top ten. I still feel the need to prove that I'm capable, that I'm responsible, that I can do this because you can survive getting horrible grades. I made it through the classes (some of them just barely), I moved through the grade levels, and I have the diplomas. Getting a 'D' in 5th grade math or failing a semester of AP World doesn't have much of an effect on my day-to-day now, but the lessons I learned and the things I internalized about myself all those years: those take longer to move past.

MY MOM, ME, & PTSD

COURTNEY BLAKE

MENTAL ILLNESS HAS ALWAYS BEEN familiar to me. My mom has
lived with depression and anxiety for most of her life. There were
days she wouldn't get out of bed, but would remain curled up
with her tattered, red robe, and a pillow over her head. My sister
and I learned to play quietly enough to not disturb her, and
managed many of our daily tasks on our own.

After years of therapy, medication management, and self-explo-
ration, I am proud to say my forty-one-year-old mother is happy,
and recently married her boyfriend of eight years. It took her a
very long time to get here. She had always told me and my sister
that she didn't want us to end up like her; a teenage mother with
only a high school degree, stuck in a toxic relationship, and a job
she hated. We vowed we would do better.

When I began exhibiting symptoms of depression at age fifteen,
I approached my dad with concerns, not wanting to worry my
mom. He responded by claiming I wasn't crazy like her. After that,
I hid in my darkness for a while. Things got significantly better
when I left my dad's house my senior year of high school to move
in with my mom and her boyfriend full-time. My mom helped me
find a therapist to see regularly, wherein I began to unpack my

anxiety, depression, and my father's abusive tendencies. My mom never shamed me for needing extra help, and she and her boyfriend provided an open, engaging, and often dysfunctional environment. I began planning my future, excitedly and mostly thrived, only to be taken down by boy issues

The summer after I graduated from high school, I was put on my first SSRI, Zoloft. I never felt shame about being on meds since my mom had always referred to her anti-depressants as her "happy pills," therefore, normalizing them. I followed suit and was convinced I would get through this. I knew I had a solid support system and endless ambition.

Everything changed.

Just a few weeks into my first year at the University of Minnesota, on September 20, 2013, I was raped by a fellow class-mate. He got me alone in my dorm room that afternoon to watch a movie. I said no repeatedly. I tried to start an argument to shift the mood, and finally I felt like I gave in. I've written about my first rape extensively on my own blog because almost three-and-a-half years later, this affects my life every single day.

I can't even describe how disgusting I felt after the assault. I had cleaned every inch of my dorm room and scrubbed my vulva until I believed there was no evidence of him on me. I waited a week to report this to my school. I waited nine days to tell my mom. I felt like telling her I had been raped would disappoint her and it would make my rape real. I was working through my mental illnesses and a breakup with my high school sweetheart; I felt I had enough on my plate.

When I told my mom, I was relieved. She and I cried over the phone. She asked me why I didn't tell her sooner, and I just sobbed harder. She attended my post-rape checkup the following day, and held my sweaty palms in her hands while I went through the re-traumatizing process of reporting my rape to the University. She reaffirmed that she was there for me, and that I could lean on her.

My perpetrator was ultimately found responsible for violating the Student Code of Conduct, and was sanctioned with mandatory counseling sessions, an essay on consent, and one year of academic probation. He violated my body, and didn't even receive a slap on the wrist. I was told I could appeal the sanctions, but was discouraged from doing so.

I felt like my life and my world had ended. I felt so much shame for not throwing him out of my dorm room, for not screaming, for not saving evidence to report to the police. My advocate at the Aurora Center, a center for victims of sexual and domestic violence, gave me words of encouragement; she told me the two common stress responses of fight or flight did not include the incredibly legitimate response of freeze.

After my assailant's sanctioning, I felt pressured to return to normal life. I became hypersexual and had sex with many men, settling with a boy who would distract me from my pain. I missed classes often, fearing I'd run into my assailant. I didn't understand the severity of panic I felt whenever encountering him. I don't know how I made it out of that semester alive, but I persisted. The only positive thing I can remember is being introduced to my mentor in the journalism school. They had been my TA in a class, and I greatly admired them. After the semester ended, they disclosed they too had a history with sexual violence. I don't know why I never expected people I practically idolized to be immune to trauma. They began to make me feel like I was not alone.

Spring semester was worse. I had no understanding of my emotions, thoughts, and behavior. I couldn't acknowledge this trauma had changed me. I occasionally had counseling sessions with a grad student at the university. She was kind, and listened to me talk about my life, but she would cry during our sessions. I began to believe I was too dark, too strange, and too much for the rest of the world. I rarely attended classes. Instead, I curled up on my boyfriend's futon all day, watching West Wing on my laptop. He noticed. Since the primary thing bringing us together was sex, we lost our connection. He broke up with me the day after Valentine's Day.

I didn't have a distraction anymore. I wallowed, I self-isolated and self-harmed. I began to plan my suicide. I felt like a burden to everyone. I knew someone who could easily provide pills that I could use to overdose. On February 25, 2014, I mentioned in my pre-counseling session survey that I was dealing with suicidal ideation. My counselor confronted me on this, and when I told her I needed her to make the decision on my hospitalization, she called my mom to pick me up and take me to the hospital.

My mom bought me lunch before she took me to the hospital. She was stoic, and she spoke to me calmly, but I could see her red, puffy eyes and the tear stains running down her face.

I was only in the hospital for a few hours. I promised I wouldn't hurt myself if I was under my mom's care. I couldn't ever do that to her. Per the psychiatrist's request, I moved back home, I withdrew from school, I began an outpatient day treatment program, and returned to the therapist I'd seen my senior year of high school.

I worked through all my therapy, because my life depended on it. I was finally given a diagnosis of Post-Traumatic Stress Disorder, but had basically no knowledge of how PTSD functioned. I hated that I wasn't in school, and felt like I was being held back. By May, I had convinced myself I was fine, and enrolled in a class for the summer, taught by my mentor. I loved the class and felt like my normal self again. For my final project, I wrote a blog post disclosing publicly that I had been sexually assaulted, and I created a YouTube video to go along with it. I received an overwhelming amount of support from my classmates and others after I went public. People from all over the country were reaching out to tell me I wasn't alone.

I returned to school full-time in the fall. On September 13, 2014, seven days before the anniversary of my first assault, I was drugged at a party, abandoned by my friends, and raped again. I found out what had happened over Facebook. An acquaintance told me I got drunk and had sex with some guy, but the guy seemed nice so it didn't matter. Then I saw a photo of most of my clothing and puke, with a caption mocking the girl who had had sex in their bedroom and threw up everywhere, wanting to hold them accountable. Since most of my belongings were at this house, I had my roommate call my mom. I was drowning in my own tears and panic. I kept screaming, "This can't happen again" repeatedly. My roommate stayed with me until my mom picked me up. She brought me to the hospital for a rape kit and stayed by my side, hugging me as I cried.

Police interviewed me. The first thing they asked was, "How do you know anything even happened?" I stopped crying, gave them a quick anatomy lesson, only to be dismissed. An investigator was assigned to my case. He barely made time for me, and I did not have the energy to fight this alone. I didn't know who raped me and whether or not they were on my campus. My mom fought for me. She made remarks that Ice-T could do a better job than my investigator. By early October, the Minneapolis Police Department declined to press charges, so I assumed the case was closed and I could at least find out the name of my perpetrator. The police department fought me at every turn. My mom and I got in contact with the head of the Sex Crimes Unit who told me he would not feel responsible for me feeling victimized. Police officers told a journalist off the record that I had been on antipsychotics, had a psychotic break, had consensual sex, and just didn't remember it.

On campus, I was often harassed by my second perpetrator's friends. My friends would continue to go to that house for parties, or spend time around those people and would attend parties at my first rapist's fraternity. They threw me a birthday party and invited two people who lived in the house and had never acknowledged what had occurred in their home. I couldn't even begin to explain my frustration and how little I began to feel about myself. Rape me once, shame on you. Rape me twice, shame on me. I began getting drunker than I normally would while going out. I had sex with many men. I consumed what I could to make me feel less empty inside.

Eight months after my initial police report, an investigator from the University of Minnesota Police Department contacted me, claiming my perpetrator had assaulted someone else. I finally had a name of my assailant. This investigator had my case transferred to him, and went back to the beginning. He re-interviewed everyone and discredited their stories. He submitted his findings to a prosecutor who declined to press charges. I felt broken. I felt like my rape wasn't violent enough to be considered rape. I developed incredibly complicated feelings while seeing other victim-survivors I cared about receive some sense of justice. Resentment boiled inside me, against my will, and I tried every day to challenge it. Some days, resentment wins.

I dropped out of the University of Minnesota for good, in the fall of 2015. What I had once considered to be my campus, had become a place where an assailant's education mattered more than a victim's. I brought bad press to the university, and I know the administration was happy to see me gone.

My mom supported my decision, as she always did. She told me she just wanted me to be well. I began EMDR with a therapist I was seeing, but wasn't stable enough to focus on it as much as I would've liked. Without school, I worked part-time in retail. I felt unfulfilled. I entered a relationship that turned toxic very quickly and has created issues between me, my family, and my friends. In October, 2016, I moved back to my mom's house after a breakdown. I have felt like a disappointment. I know I have hurt my mom. She has become exasperated, claiming she doesn't know what to do with me, and expressing her fears that I might never be a functioning adult. She has, on more than one occasion, threatened to make me homeless. This isn't the relationship I am used to.

The best explanation I could give my mom, in an effort to repair our relationship, was to talk about what PTSD has done to me. I wrote her a letter because I knew I wouldn't be able to have this conversation without bursting into tears. I told her being diagnosed with PTSD is like being diagnosed with a brain tumor. It alters your brain function, which is even visible on brain scans. Healthcare providers don't always have enough information to cure it. Progress in treatment isn't always linear. Recovery is a fight for your life.

I've begun looking into PTSD from more of a research standpoint. I know what my triggers are, and I understand I was traumatized. I need to begin to understand how this has affected me neurologically so I can be fully armed to fight this. I completed another 3-month bout of outpatient therapy, I am seeing an individual therapist weekly, and seeking out support groups of other victim-survivors. I don't quite know where I'll go from here, but I'm not going down without a fight.

DEAR DEPRESSION

JOSEPH PENOLA

Dear Depression,

I need you to know that you are not me.

Your incessant insults may make me briefly believe that I am all ofthe terrible things you tell me,but I capital-K Know that I am none of them.

I am worthy of love.

I am strong.

I am handsome.

I am enough.

The weak, ugly, unlovable monster you portray me as in the funhouse mirrors of my mind is lie, and no matter how many times you tell it to me, it will never be true.

You are going to keep talking, and I wish I could refuse to listen, but we share a body, so that's no an option.

Despite being housed in the same shell, we are different.

Your voice is not mine.

I am not you.

Sincerely,

Joseph

* * *

Weakling,

How dare you question me!

You don't deserve the voice you think you have.

Stop pretending you are separate from me.

We are one and the same.

This voice you think you have is an illusion.

You are the liar.

To believe you are anything other than what I tell you will only delude you and lead to false hope.

Listen to me if you want to stay safe.

This husk you briefly allow yourself to proud of is a prison, and the only way out is blood.

Your throat demands to be emptied of it.

Listen to me if you want to escape the pain.

My voice is the only voice.

Your Master

* * *

Dear Depression,

I am tempted to rage in response,

but I am a peaceful warrior and my confidence is strong enough without

needing to yell as you do.

I know that screaming will only fuel your fire and burn our mind.

Yes, our mind.

Not yours.

Not mine.

Ours.

I refuse to believe you are me,

but I also refuse to believe don't exist.

I've tried pretending I don't hear you.

I tried drowning you out with drugs and alcohol, only to watch you

breathe bourbon and swim.

When I resist, you persist,

so now I choose to swim with you.

I have the power of choice.

I get to choose, not you.

You will always be hungry, but I am the one who chooses whether or not I want to feed you.

You have been thriving on a diet of despair and anger. But now have a hunger for hope and so I will ingest inspiration and love, and let all of the lies I used to lap up rot.

You can rant and rave all you want, but I don't have to listen to you. I can choose whether or not I want to.

I can choose to thank you for sharing instead indulging your lies.

I can choose gratitude instead of resentment.

I can choose love instead of hate.

So I choose to see you as a blessing, instead of a curse.

And I choose to be proud of my scars instead of embarrassed by them.

You want me to believe that they are cracks that make me broken, but I am in no need of fixing, and those cracks allow others to see the light in me that you have tried so desperately to suffocate in darkness.

You have tried to convince me that I'm a mistake, but I now know that I'm a gift.

Thank you for showing me that.

BRANDON HA

I WAS STANDING THERE, head lowered down as low as it could possibly go. The bailiff had just told me to rise as some honorable judge made his way through the courtroom and took a seat on his iron throne. Not a single fuck was given. That day, as the antipsychotic medication I'd been forcibly given over the past few weeks had finally started to take effect, all I could think about was how I got here. Not just the local county court in San Jose that day, but at thirty, hitting the lowest of the low and achieving almost nothing in my life. I was a failure, simple as that. And I didn't know how to dig my way out. There was no road map to seek for directions; it seemed like no one knew anything about mental illness. I'd have to do it alone and I was scared shitless.

When I was first diagnosed in 2002 with bipolar disorder (well, the shrink called it manic depression at the time), I didn't know how to feel. There I was, in the psych hospital and this old doctor told me I had manic depression.

"Excuse me, what? What's manic depression?" I asked

"Well, people call it bipolar disorder these days," he replied.

"Wtf is that?" still confused as hell.

After informing me about it being, explaining that it's a mood condition and that I'd temporarily (hah!) need to take three types of medications including an antipsychotic, mood stabilizer, and antidepressant, I'd be okay. Quite the cocktail, but I should do what the doctor orders, I guess. So, I was released from the hospital and had a treatment plan: take my meds and continually see a psychiatrist and therapist. Over the next few months, things did begin to look up. I was able to get a cushy job at a hi-tech company through a college buddy and thought I was well on my way to living a normal life, whatever the hell that meant. No one had to know about my stint in the psych hospital and definitely not about my manic bipolar whatever it was called, diagnosis. Secrecy was my motto and I made damn sure I kept it.

So, there I am, living the dream kinda...sorta. Somehow, I miraculously by the grace of God was able to save enough money to afford buying a new condo in the Bay Area just four years after my hospitalization. That meant I was cured, right? I hadn't been on meds and seen anyone for therapy for a long time prior, and buying a house was the ultimate definition of adulting; I can't adult if I'm crazy. I was no doctor, but I was cured. It was a gut feeling and that intuition is never, ever wrong.

Right.

Now, I have this new place with a fat mortgage and stupid HOA payments. Welcome to adulthood, also known as, the land of unbearable stress and lack of proper coping mechanisms. How did I deal with the unwelcome triggers to a mood disorder? By responsibly checking up with a psychiatrist or therapist and telling them exactly what I was experiencing? Absolutely not. I'm not crazy and I'm not seeing a shrink again. I'm just going to do what every other red-blooded (Asian) American would do: seek solace with my best friend, Jack Daniel's. It was the only form of medication that worked, temporarily or not.

That year, in 2006, I once again returned to the psych hospital. This time was much different than the first, though. I owned a home, had a decent paying job, and had great people around me. Life was good. So, when I eventually became hospitalized for a manic episode, I was beyond devastated. The embarrassment of people finally knowing I was crazy was too much to bear. The depression sunk into this black pit where I saw absolutely no glimpse of light. I tried to take my life, not once but twice. I obviously failed at that, so now I'm this super-duper failure that can't do anything right.

I wish I could tell you I had an epiphany after my two attempts, but I can't. Unfortunately, the entirety of my twenties can be summed up in one word: shame. And that day, when I was in court, I never felt any lower. For most people living with bipolar disorder and don't take the necessary steps for treatment, each manic/depressive episode gets worse and worse. Four months prior to my infamous day in court, I was sober, taking classes at a local community college, and as stable as I'd ever been before. I was even at my peak, physically, and just finished my first half-marathon in one hour, fifty-one minutes, and four seconds. But the night I turned thirty, I went to Vegas to celebrate, foolishly thinking I was strong enough to avoid the temptation of my biggest trigger, Mr. JD.

I took a shot of the dark stuff and it triggered my *Fear and Loathing in Las Vegas* moment for four long months. This episode was different.

Instead of being the annoying douche with an abundance of energy and crazy (sometimes incredible) ideas, I was psychotic. Remember 2007 Britney? Well I was a few notches above that. One of the delusions I experienced, was hearing voices. Those whispers in my ears were so vivid, and so real that I thought there was no way they weren't there. These voices had some serious mind control abilities and told me race cars on the highway, and that I'd graduated from law school, as well as, to go steal things. Normally, my episodes lasted a few short weeks, but this went on for what seemed like forever. And like Winona Ryder knows, once you start stealing things, you're bound to get caught. I did and that's how I landed in court.

That day, when I was at my absolute lowest of the low, sitting in court listening to other cases involving DUIs and assaults, I was a shell of whoever my former self was. I didn't know who the fuck I was, but there was one thing for sure—Iwas crazy. No ifs, ands, or buts. None. There is no worse feeling than coming out of that cloudy, post-psychosis haze and becoming self-aware that I was a loser, especially in a courtroom. I sat there with my mom who dealt with the hospitalizations and arrests like a champion as she had throughout my entire life. When Captain Cool becomes Captain Crazy, people start to distance themselves from your life real quick—not my gangster mom though, who's dealt with the loss of two husbands and her own life tragedies. With my head down, on the verge of tears, she put her hand on mine and said, "Huy (my Vietnamese name), whatever you do, no matter how many times you think you've failed, I will always love you."

My heart was officially broken. Sounds light some cliché Nicholas Sparks movie shit, right? It does, I know. But that's what fueled my recovery with bipolar disorder and alcoholism. I haven't had a drop to drink since February 24, 2010, and though I've had my fair share of ups and downs along this journey, I'm still fighting—for me, for my community with *Break Yo Stigma*, and especially for my mama.

But if research determines mental illness is hereditary, I'm definitely blaming her.

EPILOGUE

BREAKING THE CYCLE

LIVING with mental illness is a challenge and an education. Learning how to navigate relationships, responsibilities, and life in general when your illness actively sabotages your plans. Additionally, society contributes its own prejudices and expectations.

Mental colonization.

Society's perspective usurping and reinterpreting one's concept of self, particularly through the lens of mental illness. Identity struggling to be self-determined in the face of stigma. When those ideas become a part of your identity, they become self-reinforcing.

The process by which we begin to rewrite our internal narratives: I am not broken, but this place, these people, this moment, is breaking me. Ownership is an important part of that process. Learning to view ourselves outside of our conditions as people with manageable flaws rather than as damaged goods.

Self-empowerment, acceptance of one's differentness and reframing it as a source of strength. Breaking the cycle by leading through example, allowing ourselves to shine and giving others the license to join in. Eight in ten people have some form of mental illness -- so why do we feel so isolated?

The reason is because society tells us that we are fundamentally wrong. The first step is to accept ourselves for who we are and be proud of that identity no matter what the societal backlash may be. It's about standing up and being proud of yourself no matter how "broken" an external institution tells you that you are.

Let's push back against these stigmas, and hopefully, soon we'll live in a more tolerant and enriched society which accepts people with mental illness.

Sarah Comerford, Vice President
and
Sarah Fader, CEO, Stigma Fighters

Made in the USA
Lexington, KY
01 February 2018